ENTERPRISE-GRADE IT SECURITY FOR SMALL AND MEDIUM BUSINESSES

BUILDING SECURITY SYSTEMS, IN PLAIN ENGLISH

Denny Cherry

Apress®

Enterprise-Grade IT Security for Small and Medium Businesses: Building Security Systems, in Plain English

Denny Cherry
Denny Cherry & Associates Consulting, LLC, Oceanside, CA, USA

ISBN-13 (pbk): 978-1-4842-8627-2
https://doi.org/10.1007/978-1-4842-8628-9

ISBN-13 (electronic): 978-1-4842-8628-9

Managing Director, Apress Media LLC: Welmoed Spahr
Acquisitions Editor: Jonathan Gennick
Development Editor: Laura Berendson
Coordinating Editor: Jill Balzano
Copy Editor: April Rondeau

Cover designed by eStudioCalamar

Cover image designed by Freepik (www.freepik.com)

Distributed to the book trade worldwide by Springer Science+Business Media New York, 1 New York Plaza, Suite 4600, New York, NY 10004-1562, USA. Phone 1-800-SPRINGER, fax (201) 348-4505, email orders-ny@springer-sbm.com, or visit www.springeronline.com. Apress Media, LLC is a California LLC and the sole member (owner) is Springer Science+Business Media Finance Inc (SSBM Finance Inc). SSBM Finance Inc is a **Delaware** corporation.

For information on translations, please e-mail booktranslations@springernature.com; for reprint, paperback, or audio rights, please e-mail bookpermissions@springernature.com.

Apress titles may be purchased in bulk for academic, corporate, or promotional use. eBook versions and licenses are also available for most titles. For more information, reference our Print and eBook Bulk Sales web page at http://www.apress.com/bulk-sales.

Any source code or other supplementary material referenced by the author in this book is available to readers on GitHub (https://github.com/Apress). For more detailed information, please visit http://www.apress.com/source-code.

Printed on acid-free paper

Thank you to my wife, Kris, for putting up with my writing another book, which I know isn't her favorite activity for me to go through. And thank you to my team at Denny Cherry & Associates Consulting who reviewed the book as well as kept me on task with both the book and our client projects that were in flight at the same time.

Contents

About the Author

Denny Cherry has been working in the information technology field for over 20 years and has written almost a dozen IT books and hundreds of articles for various publications, including *Inc.*, *MSDN* magazine, and *SQL Server* magazine, as well as spoken at dozens of conferences around the world. He holds the Microsoft Certified Master certification, has been awarded the Microsoft Most Valuable Professional (MVP) award annually for over 15 years, and has been awarded the VMware vExpert award six times. His public speaking started at local events in Southern California where he lives with his wife and their pet rabbits, and has expanded out to events worldwide. Speaking at conferences has taken Denny to six continents and over a dozen countries, where he speaks at both small local events and large industry and corporate events.

About the Technical Reviewer

Paul Cretaro is an information technology professional with over 25 years of industry experience, mostly concentrated in information security and team management. He has been CISSP certified for over 18 years and is an ISC2 subject matter expert for the CISSP exam. He has strong managerial skills with extensive training experience. Paul is an MCSE Windows expert, college-level trainer, and published author, with hands-on security lab manuals sold worldwide. Paul has also worked in the financial sector for 16 years, supporting information technology and security.

Introduction

With *Enterprise-Grade IT Security for Small and Medium Businesses*, I wanted to take a different approach than most IT books. Most are written with the assumption that the reader knows what they should put in place, and they are a sort of how-to book on implementing the various solutions. With *Enterprise-Grade IT Security for Small and Medium Businesses*, the approach was instead taken to educate people who don't normally work hands-on with these various technologies. Thus, executives can have a good understanding of what technology solutions are available, and can ask questions of their IT teams as to why don't they have X, and do they need to have Y in place, while having an understanding of what these technology solutions are capable of doing.

In Chapter 1, we'll review why IT security matters and why companies need to have an IT security infrastructure in place. One of the big reasons why companies don't invest in IT security is because it is expensive, and often the company doesn't see the benefit to spending the money.

In Chapter 2, we will take a slightly more technical approach as we talk about network design decisions that companies can make for how their network is designed. These range from fairly wide open with all the devices on the network able to communicate with all the other devices, to a network that is segmented, preventing devices on the network from accessing other devices unless specific access is granted.

In Chapter 3, we will review what firewalls are, what they do, and why are they useful for companies to deploy to protect their network infrastructure. This will include the cloud options available in the three major clouds.

In Chapter 4, we will review denial of services and distributed denial of service attacks, and how they are prevented using distributed denial of service appliances. We'll also compare and contrast these appliances with firewalls so that we can see when one is used versus the other. This will include the cloud options available in the three major clouds.

In Chapter 5, we will review the remote connectivity options that companies can make available to their users, including why they are good to have and the risks that these solutions introduce.

In Chapter 6, we will review the security options available within each of the major operating systems. This includes why the various platforms should be patched and upgraded frequently.

In Chapter 7, we will review what multi-factor authentication is, how it should be used, and when it should be used.

In Chapter 8, we will learn about zero trust environments and how companies can benefit from having such an environment in their network infrastructure.

In Chapter 9, we will talk about the weakest link in IT security—the company staff. We will review the training that employees should be doing regularly, as well as what topics should be covered in that training.

In Chapter 10, we will continue on this theme of employee training to not only secure their company resources but also their daily life, as an attacker's gaining access to personal resources can be leveraged to compromise the employee's business life.

The Infrastructure

Why IT Security Matters

Information technology (IT) security is one of the most ignored parts of IT. IT security should be considered a subset of physical security. When it is, the company is much less likely to ignore IT security processes. You wouldn't leave the company's front door unlocked, and IT security should have the same level of attention paid to it.

When a company builds a new application, and the budget gets tight, cuts have to be made. For many companies, IT security is one of the first things to be cut from the project. There is a simple reason for this: security costs money and doesn't typically add to the bottom line. When pitching an application to customers, the security of the application won't close the deal, and when the development process goes over budget the security review can potentially get cut to save money.

IT security has many different goals. While the most obvious one is to protect the computer network, and therefore the business, from outside attack, that is only one of the goals of a proper IT security configuration. It also needs to support the business in general. If the business isn't able to sell widgets because the IT security is too complex and too secure, then the security infrastructure hasn't been properly built. IT security's primary goal is to protect the company, while allowing the business needs to be accomplished.

D. Cherry, *Enterprise-Grade IT Security for Small and Medium Businesses*,
https://doi.org/10.1007/978-1-4842-8628-9_1

All too often IT security personnel forget about that second part of what they need to do. The security personnel focus on the best ways to secure the environment without considering the needs of the business users to complete their day-to-day work. Considering these needs does not make IT security easier; in fact, it often makes the process of securing the network from bad actors much harder.

There is an adage in IT, and that is that the only truly secure computer is the one that is turned off and unplugged. And to some extent this is true. A computer that is powered off (and unplugged) *probably* can't be compromised. For additional security, that powered-off computer could be unplugged and placed in a cinderblock room with no doors and no windows. Then it would probably be secure enough, until someone comes by with a jack hammer and a power cord. Now suddenly our computer is a lot less secure than it was before.

The problem with putting all of the computers, powered off, in a windowless, doorless concrete room is that we can't get any work done. So, a happy medium has to be found between a powered-off, locked-up computer and a computer that's just sitting on the internet with no protection.

As we will do throughout this book, we're going to review and demystify a variety of IT security concepts so that when you, the company executive, are talking to your IT staff, you will have a firm grasp of what they are talking about, what they are recommending be implemented, and why they want to implement those features and products. And, most important, you will recognize that they are talking about *not* implementing specific measures, and you'll be able to ask them why they feel that those measures do not need to be taken.

As we move through the book, we'll be covering some network design patterns that have the best success rate at preventing intrusion into the company, from both attacks that start from within the company as well as those that start from the outside the company. From there, we'll look at firewall appliances as well as appliances designed to protect against distributed denial of service (DDOS) attacks, which are coordinated attacks against a company's infrastructure by thousands of computers across the internet.

From there, we'll move into remote connectivity, which will need to take features like network design into account to allow users to work remotely. While the need to work remotely is extremely important during a pandemic like the Covid-19 pandemic of 2019 to 2022 and beyond, working remotely is and has been a reality of IT work for decades at this point, even if it hasn't been for the other employees at the company. IT workers need to be able to work from anywhere, because if there's a problem with the servers or the network, they need to be able to resolve those issues quickly and from anywhere, and the work they are doing must be protected and not exposed to bad actors.

As we move into Part II of this book, we'll review the various operating systems that are available, the debate among the zealots who preach for each operating system platform, and which one is the best option for the enterprise.

We'll review what multi-factor authentication is, when it should be used, and, most important, how it should be used and how it can and has failed people. Learning from the mistakes of others is how we learn about those gaps in security.

We'll wrap up Part II with a concept that is taking foothold in IT today: zero-trust environments. In a zero-trust environment, we trust no one and nothing until it has proven itself. We'll explore this topic in depth and talk through when this should be used and what the benefits are.

In Part III of this book, we're going to move away from the technical solutions that govern the daily lives of IT workers, and move toward the weakest link in IT security, the company employees who can, and sadly often do, allow breaches to happen within the environment.

We'll start off by reviewing the protections that we can put in front of people to prevent bad actors' getting to them at all. We'll finish off by talking about employee training that should be happening regularly and frequently to ensure that the employees aren't being unwitting vectors, allowing a breach of the company network without realizing it.

Why We Need IT Security

The internet is much like the wild, wild west of the 1800s. Without IT security, the internet is basically a free-for-all where people will attack anything that they can, often with the goal of being able to brag about what they were able to do. At least, that's the way things used to be back in the early internet days in the 1990s (don't forget, time in technology feels much faster than actual time). In the modern world, without proper IT security in place our companies are wide open for abuse by bad actors who want to steal customer data for the purpose of selling it to the highest bidder. Additionally, bad actors can hold companies' information for ransom until the company either pays the ransom or the attacker gives up and deletes the key that is used to unlock the information.

Customers trust the companies that they do business with, as they expect the companies to guard their personal information. As companies, we need to do a better job of protecting that information. Even in the most innocuous of circumstances customers are providing us with their username, password, email address, and name. While having access to just an email address, name, and a password wouldn't get a bad actor all the information needed to commit identity theft, it would get them a lot closer.

Now assume that you collect some additional information for a customer, including their current address and birthday. With this information (for U.S. customers, at least) I can come shockingly close to figuring out what the person's Social Security number is. And with that, I can commit identity theft.

The way that an address can be translated into a Social Security number is fairly straightforward. The first thing to remember is that over 70 percent of Americans live in, or close to, the city in which they grew up, according to a report from North American Van Lines, which is available at `https:// egits4smb.com/go/avl`.

■ **Note** All the URLs in this book will refer to the web page that has been set up for this book, which is `www.egits4smb.com`. These URLs will be shorter and easier to type then the actual websites that hold the information for these references. These URLs will simply refer you to the correct location for this information.

The next piece of information to remember is that Social Security numbers (SSNs) were given out in batches to hospitals, and it was recorded which batches were given out where. This process changed in June 2011, when the Social Security department started assigning random numbers, but from the inception of the Social Security number in the 1930s until June 2011, Social Security numbers could be guessed fairly easily.

■ **Note** Seventy percent of Americans live in, or close to, the city in which they grew up.

By looking at the Social Security department's website, specifically at `https:// egits4smb.com/go/stateweb`, we can see what the first three numbers should be for a person based on the state that they currently live in (knowing that they probably haven't left the state that they were born in). We can then look at the high group information to see what the range of values were for the second number for those SSNs distributed in the year of issue (and birth for most people). The information can be found again on the Social Security department's website, at `https://egits4smb.com/go/ssnv`. We've now successfully narrowed down the SSN from ~1 billion possibilities to 1,000 possibilities.

With a little bit of digging into various data dumps from companies that have been breached in the past, I could probably find the final four digits of a person's Social Security number. This is because many companies and websites will collect this information for verification purposes, and often those companies will store the last four digits of the Social Security number in plain text, which would give the potential attacker everything that they need to steal the customer's identity.

Because of the relative ease with which critical information can be figured out, protecting this information is critical to the success of a company.

When the customer's information is compromised, the customer loses faith in the company, and that faith in the company can take months or years to earn back, if ever. Because of this, we need to keep our customers' data safe.

From a company perspective, companies don't want to lose the faith of the public. This is especially true of public companies that rely on the general public to purchase the public stock of the company. A simple example of this can be seen by reviewing the SolarWinds breach, which was announced on December 8, 2020. We can see in Figure 1-1 how the stock price fell rapidly on December 9 and 10.

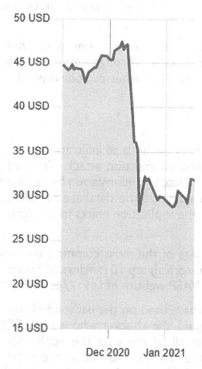

Figure 1-1. SolarWinds stock price in December 2020 and January 2021

As of the writing of this book in August 2022, the SolarWinds stock price has yet to recover, and we can therefore assume consumer confidence in SolarWinds hasn't yet either. It should be noted that when reviewing the SolarWinds stock price, there was a stock split on July 30, 2021, which needs to be taken into account.

Because of this reality, companies need to be constantly reviewing their practices and protocols to ensure that a weakness hasn't come into existence since the protocols were put in place.

When IT security is correctly implemented, the information that the company holds will be safe and secure, and the company's employees will be able to do the job that they need to complete in order to help the company succeed. Properly implemented IT security will usually cause employees to hate the IT security team, and having proper security in place will cause slowdowns when users are starting their work, but this is the nature of IT security.

Types of Attacks on Companies

There are a variety of attack vectors an attacker can use to infiltrate a company's network. While attackers will generally have one specific type they use most often, a company will need to protect itself against all of the attack vectors.

In this section, we'll examine some of the most common attack vectors and how these breaches can occur. Throughout the rest of this book we'll be covering how these potential breaches can be stopped.

SQL Injection

One of the most common methods of infiltration into a company's network starts with what is called an injection attack. With an injection attack the attacker is able to manipulate the information being sent through a web form in a website in such a way that the database or middleware server that is running the backend of the application reacts to the command differently than the developer expects.

While the annual rankings of the most common security risks change every year, the current (and historical) top 10 rankings of the common security issues are available on the OWASP website `https://egits4smb.com/go/owasp`.

Depending on the database used on the backend of the application, and how the application is designed, the attacker who is using SQL injection is able to either export some or all of the data the application uses, or force the database server to install software that allows the attacker to use this server as a jumping-off point to infiltrate and attack the rest of the company's servers and workstations.

SQL injection is a very popular way for bad actors to breach companies' networks as the entire process can be scripted and left to run against a specific target, or against an entire range of IP addresses on the internet.

The core reason that SQL injection exists is due to errors in the development process that go unnoticed by either the developers or the quality assurance (QA) process. These errors in the application don't change the way the application functions, which is why they aren't found.

The only reliable way to find these SQL injection flaws is to use SQL injection as part of the QA process to ensure that everything is working correctly and that a SQL injection attack wouldn't be successful. However, adding this step to the QA process is often expensive and time-consuming, which will slow down the release cycle of applications, potentially greatly.

Adding this testing process to the QA cycle will only affect applications under current development. Often, SQL injection attacks are successful against new applications as the developers know what needs to be done to ensure that SQL injection isn't successful. The applications that were developed 10–20 years ago, however, which are still published on the internet, sometimes without anyone at the company realizing that they are so published, are more open to attack.

Another class of application that might be susceptible to a SQL injection attack is vendor-provided applications. While vendors of applications mean well, their applications are often not fully tested for SQL injection attack vulnerabilities. Even if they are tested, what proof do vendors offer besides their word that the application is fully tested?

Credential Hijacking

Another common method of gaining unauthorized access to computer networks is through credential hijacking. The underlying method here is that a bad actor gets the username and password of an employee, and that username and password are used to gain access to network resources that the bad actor is able to exploit.

There are two basic methods for getting credentials. The first is a brute-force attack in which the attacker tries every possible combination of values until a successful combination is found. This is a very time-consuming method and will typically not be successful unless the bad actor has the username of the employee, in which case they just need to keep trying passwords until they are successful.

The second method, which is typically more successful, is to simply trick the employee into giving over their password in some way. This can be done in a few different ways, from emails that look legitimate, such as the ever popular "your password has expired" emails, or other official-looking emails, all of which have the same goal of getting the reader to click the link, which will then prompt them for their corporate username and password.

Another method that is often successful but requires more time and effort on the part of the bad actor is to use social engineering. Social engineering requires contacting the target of the attack, often by phone, and attempting to get the target to give up internal information. Sometimes the goal of the attack isn't to gain the username and password of the target, but rather more information about the internal workings of the company. In fact, some hacker conferences, such as the Def Con conference, host social engineering attack contests. While there are no recordings of the calls at such contests (due to U.S. federal wiretapping laws), a re-enactment of one such call can be found at https://egits4smb.com/go/social. While the recording is a few years old, it is a great example of the techniques that can be used, which haven't changed all that much since the recording was made in 2018.

As you can see in the video, the victim didn't give their username or password, but they gave the attacker a wealth of information about the retail location and about the company in general. Once information about the company is gathered, another member of the staff could be contacted to attempt to get them to give over their username and password. If the contacted employee won't give over their password, the attacker can work on resetting the employee's password. This involves getting various pieces of information from the employee that seem rather innocuous, such as the name of the employee's first pet, type of car for their first car, etc.

A perfect example of social engineering's being successful involves social networking giant Twitter, when in July 2020 a employee's username and password were given to an attacker by the Twitter employee. The attacker was able to bypass the multi-factor authentication in place on the account (we'll talk more about multi-factor authentication later in this book). Once they were connected to the administrative screens of the Twitter websites, the attacker was able to successfully send tweets using 130 accounts of high-profile users of Twitter, including President Barack Obama, President Joe Biden (when he was vice president), as well as a variety of world-renowned business leaders, such as Elon Musk, Bill Gates, and Jeff Bezos.

Internal Attacks

One of the hardest attack vectors to eliminate is the internal attack. This is an attack by a company employee, contractor, or other person who is authorized to be inside the building. When the person is outside of the environment, a straightforward approach can be taken to ensure that they don't get inside the network. However, when the bad actor is physically inside the building, things get much harder to deal with.

For internal attacks, we need to consider network ports that don't have computers plugged into them, USB ports on computers, and whether the employees are happy and thus aren't going to take customer data from the systems.

■ **Note**   Back when I worked at an internet service provider in the late 1990s and early 2000s, it was shocking to see just how much confidential information executives and managers would leave sitting on their desks in their offices, assuming that it was secure.

At about 6 p.m., all the managers and above would leave, locking their office doors on their way out. At about 7 p.m. the building security personnel would come through and unlock every office and prop the doors open so that the cleaning crew could get into all of the offices. When they were done at about 11 p.m., the security guards would come through and close all the doors and ensure that they were locked up tight.

While the building security staff didn't have keys to the server rooms, that wasn't needed, as every executive's office was wide open for hours, and if someone had come in with the cleaning crew and sat in an office for a few hours, no one would have ever known.

IT Security Is Expensive: Is It Worth the Cost?

The short answer to the question of "Is IT security worth the cost?" is yes. Properly implemented IT security is worth every penny that's been paid for it, and more. A perfect example of this can be found at https://www.egits4smb.com/go/long-haul, where the 2020 attack of CMA CGN in France ended up costing the company $50 million or more. Properly implemented IT may have cost the company $5 million, allowing them to save $45 million. And this doesn't include the cost of a future attack on the company—and that future attack is going to come. The attackers have, by being successful in an attack, proven that they can break into the company and get something worth getting.

Many companies are attacked by ransomware groups repeatedly. The companies that have paid the ransomware groups to unlock data being held for ransom have proven that they are willing to pay such ransoms. This tells the ransomware group that if they hold the company's data for ransom again in a few months, the company will pay the ransom again. There are companies that are held for ransom once or twice a year and forced to pay millions of dollars for each ransom event.

By investing in proper IT security, these ransomware events would be stopped and the company wouldn't be forced to choose between paying the ransom and losing all their information.

One of the problems with the cost of IT security is that when IT security is done correctly and there are no breaches to the infrastructure, the IT security costs look like a waste of money. But that isn't the case at all. When IT security is doing its job, there should be no successful breaches. This doesn't mean that IT security spending needs to be reduced; instead, it means that IT security is working correctly.

When a company doesn't invest in their IT security, they are just asking to be exploited. Even when companies *do* invest in IT security, it doesn't guarantee that they won't be attacked by a bad actor. One of the ways in which companies are able to protect themselves is by making themselves look uninviting. This is done by making attacking the company so hard and so expensive that the bad actor looks for a cheaper and easier victim to attack.

When bad actors are going to attack a company, they perform a cost-benefit analysis similar to that business executives do—they just may not realize it. "Am I going to make enough money from this attack to cover the costs of doing it, and still make money to feed myself and my family?" If the answer to this question is "no" then there's no point in attacking the company, if the answer is "yes" then the attack on the company can start.

If the IT security is minimal or non-existent, then the cost to the attacker to attempt to infiltrate the company is low, and the odds of success are high. If, however, the company has good IT security in place, and the company is difficult to breach, or it will take months of dedicated work to break into the company, then the attacker will move on as there are easier companies to break into.

Not every aspect of IT security is expensive. Just as USB was being introduced to computers, IT security workers were discovering a problem with USB ports in a corporate environment. They would automatically mount and run whatever USB device was inserted into them. This is a great feature for the home user who isn't an IT expert and who doesn't know how to mount a device on their computer to access it. But this suddenly left enterprise computers with a brand-new massive vulnerability. When USB was first introduced there was no enterprise solution to turn off the USB ports, short of opening every computer and very carefully unsoldering the USB ports from the motherboard to remove them. There needed to be a better solution. There in fact was, and that solution was glue. Glue was inserted into the USB ports on the computers so that the ports couldn't be used. Once glue dries it doesn't conduct electricity, so there was no worry of the USB ports shorting themselves out. It's a low-tech solution for a high-tech problem, and one that's still in use today at some companies that don't have an enterprise-wide solution to disable the USB ports on their computers.

Defense in Depth

One of the phrases that you will hear mentioned by IT security professionals is "defense in depth." The idea behind defense in depth is that people get only the access that they need to complete their job, no more and no less. This often rubs executives the wrong way, especially at smaller companies. This is because executives at smaller companies, especially company owners, feel that they should have access to everything at the company. While this is an understandable feeling to have, it doesn't follow the best IT security practices, as it gives one person access to more systems than they need.

Oftentimes business owners don't need access to all the folders on the company file share, or access to all the internal servers. If an executive has access to everything within the organization, and the executive's account is compromised, the bad actor could gain access to every server in the company.

This—combined with the fact that company executives are typically public figures with their names and possibly email addresses listed on the company website—makes executives an easy target for bad actors. Were a bad actor to complete a spear-phishing campaign against the executive, the odds are that the campaign would eventually be successful. Even executives who didn't think that they would be targets, could be targets.

■ **Note** Several years ago a company executive was sent a spear-phishing email. The executive was security savvy; however, he still clicked on the link in the email. The executive happened to be purchasing something from a friend and was expecting an email from the friend. The spear-phishing email happened to be from the friend's email address.

Thankfully the executive figured out that it was a phishing email very quickly, and the bad actor who sent the email wasn't able to log on to the company's network, access the executive's email account, or install anything on the executive's laptop. It was a very close call.

Defense in depth is a solid technique for ensuring that when an account is compromised, that account can't compromise an entire company. While it is annoying to need to request access to files or systems at a company at which you are an executive, security isn't about making accessing files and systems easier. IT security resolves around ensuring that when an account is compromised, the least amount of company property is affected. One of the things that must be done is to assume that everyone's account will be compromised, and at the worst possible time.

By taking this approach, we ensure that we are building our systems and processes so that employees, executives, and business owners have access to the fewest company systems as possible.

Specific Security Compliance Standards

On top of the general best practices and security standards that will be discussed throughout this book, there are a variety of specific security standards that companies may or may not be held to depending on what business they are in, and how they conduct their business.

■ **Note**   All of the information about these compliance standards was current as of early 2022. These compliance standards may have changed since that date. It is recommended that these standards be reviewed with your CFO, in-house legal team, and/or accountant to examine which compliance standards apply to your company and ensure current accuracy of the information presented in this section, as these standards change more frequently then a book can be updated.

FedRamp

The United States federal government has a security standard called FedRamp that all government suppliers and government systems are held to. This includes any cloud vendors that are hosting services used by the United States government. To meet this requirement, Microsoft Azure has been split into three different cloud platforms.

The most common Microsoft Azure platform is the commercial cloud, which is typically referred to as Microsoft Azure. This cloud platform, while extremely secure, does not meet the FedRamp requirements.

The second portion of the Microsoft Azure platform is commonly known as the Microsoft Azure Government Cloud Computing platform (GCC). This platform does meet the FedRamp requirements and is completely separate from the commercial Microsoft Azure platform. The GCC environment has its own Microsoft Azure regions as well as a dedicated Microsoft Azure portal. While the commercial cloud is managed via `https://portal.azure.com`, the GCC environment is managed from `https://portal.azure.us`. The GCC has features such as network peering, which does work between virtual networks in Microsoft Azure and within GCC, but does not work where one virtual network is in Microsoft Azure and the second one is within the GCC environment.

The third portion of the Microsoft Azure platform is the Microsoft Azure Department of Defense (DoD) cloud platform. This environment goes beyond the FedRamp requirements and is considered to be the most secure of the Microsoft Azure platforms.

Usage of the GCC platform is limited to U.S. federal and state government employees who have a .gov email address as well as U.S. federal and state government vendors who are sponsored by a government employee.

Usage of the DoD platform is limited to the same requirements; however, employees who sign up for the DoD platform must be working for the Department of Defense or be a vendor for the Department of Defense.

All of the requirements of the FedRamp program are published online and can be viewed at `https://egits4smb.com/go/fedramp`.

SOC

SOC, which stands for System and Organizations Controls, is a framework used in a variety of industries to assist with securing servers and systems within the company. SOC as a framework was built by the American Institute of CPAs (AICPA) and is used to help ensure that companies are providing the availability and security they claim to be providing. Depending on the report type, which is produced as part of an SOC review, the report may be for internal use only, or it may be designed for external use to be shared with customers and vendors as needed.

The SOC framework has three different levels, each building on the prior. These frameworks are known as SOC 1, SOC 2, and SOC 3.[1] At their core these frameworks ensure that there are proper controls in place to confirm that the company has properly examined and certified that the controls and processes that are in place are sufficient for the work being done by the company.

SOC 1

SOC 1 is a report on controls that are in place at a service organization relevant to user entities' internal controls over financial reports (ECFR). The reports the company and its auditors produce are prepared in accordance with AT-C section 320, specifically the section *Reporting on an Examination of Controls at a Service Organization Relevant to User Entities' Internal Control Over Financial Reporting.* These reports are designed to ensure that the company in question meets the requirements of SOC 1 and that a certified public accountant (CPA) has audited the financial statements of the company to ensure that the statements are accurate.

SOC 1 reports fall into one of two types: Type 1 or Type 2. Type 1 reports report on the fairness of management's description of the organization's systems and the suitability of the design of the controls in relation to the statement objectives of those controls as of the specified date within the report. What this means in plain English is that the plans and controls that the company has in place will do what the company says that they will do, as of whatever date the company says that they will do them.

Type 2 reports build on the information provided in Type 1 reports, adding the phrase "and operating effectiveness" to the requirements of the reports. This means that Type 2 reports report on the fairness of management's description of the organization's systems and the suitability of the design and operating effectiveness of the controls in relation to the statement objectives of those controls as of the specified date within the report. What this means

---

[1] SOC 1, SOC 2, and SOC 3 are registered trademarks of AICPA.

in plain English is that the plans and controls that the company has in place will do what the company says that they will do, and that they've been tested, as of whatever date the company says that they will do them.

SOC 1 reports are considered confidential, and they are not for distribution.

SOC 2

SOC 2 reporting is the version most commonly used as it is required by credit card processors for any company that holds credit card information within the systems of the company.

SOC 2 reports are intended to report on the controls at the company related to the security, availability, and processing integrity of the systems that the company uses to process users' data and the confidentiality and privacy of the information processed by these systems. This means that any systems that store or process customer information must be included on the SOC 2 report.

Many companies that have systems that must be included in a SOC 2 report will have two sperate production environments. One of those environments will contain the systems that are SOC 2 compliant, and the other environment will not require SOC 2 auditing and reporting. These two environments will be totally independent from each other, as a complete line in the sand must be drawn; otherwise, the systems that don't fall within the SOC 2 audit will fall under the SOC 2 umbrella.

SOC 2 reports are considered confidential, and they are not for distribution.

SOC 3

SOC 3 reports are similar to SOC 2 reports, but are designed to be read and understood by someone who doesn't have the specific domain knowledge required to make effective use of an SOC 2 report. The SOC 3 reports detail the controls at the organization regarding the security, availability, processing integrity confidentiality, and privacy of the organization.

Unlike SOC 1 and SOC 2 reports, SOC 3 reports can be distributed to customers, users, etc.

More information about the various SOC services and controls is available at https://egits4smb.com/go/soc.

ISO/IEC 27001

The ISO/IEC 27001 Information Technology Security techniques, Information security management systems requirements is a standard that specifies the *requirements for establishing, implementing, operating, monitoring, reviewing, maintaining and improving a documented information security management system within the context of the business activities of the organization and the risks it faces. — SC27 Standing Document 11 (2021)*

The requirements found within the ISO/IEC 27001 document are not meant to give the company a specific list of software to be installed and how it should be configured. Instead, this document gives companies a list of end goals to meet; what the company determines to implement and how the company determines to implement those solutions are completely up to the company, so long as the end result of the implementation is that the solution meets the requirements of ISO/IEC 27001 and the solution is compliant with the guidelines. One reason for this openness as to what needs to be implemented is the fact that the writers of the ISE/IEC 27001 document understood that the specific controls that are needed vary widely between industries and specific administrators' capabilities. While one company may implement "Solution X" on the Linux platform, that solution may not be the best solution for another company, especially if that company has all of its servers based on the Windows operating system instead of the Linux platform.

ISO/IEC 27001 serves two purposes. The first is to provide for the design of an information security management system (ISMS). The second purpose is the basis for formal compliance, which requires an audit by an accredited auditor to ensure that the organization is compliant with ISO/IEC 27001. While an audit of compliance is not needed for every organization, it is often required by potential customers and/or suppliers to ensure that any information trusted to the company will be properly secured.

While not every company needs to complete the audit process, most if not all companies should hold themselves to the standards laid out within the ISO/IEC 27001 requirements.

As part of the ISO/IER 27001 certification process, there are 15 items that require documentation to be collected. This documentation can be printed on paper, but more often is stored within some sort of online collaboration tool, such as a Wiki or SharePoint solution that the company already has in place. This allows the document history to be tracked over time as changes to the document are made, which is a requirement of the standard. Online systems are recommended in this day and age as changes between versions of the documents can be more easily tracked, along with documentation regarding who made the changes.

More information about ISO/IEC 27001 can be found online at https://egits4smb.com/go/27001.

Microsoft Operational Security Assurance Practices

The Microsoft corporation has published the Microsoft Operational Security Assurance practices (OSA) with the end goal of assisting companies to improve operational security within cloud-based infrastructures.

The OSA discusses many of the same techniques that are discussed throughout the remaining chapters of this book. These practices include the following:

1. End-user training (Chapter 10)

2. Using multi-factor authentication (Chapter 7)

3. Least privilege (Chapter 9)

4. Protecting secrets (Chapter 9)

5. Minimizing the attack surface (Chapter 6)

6. Encrypting data in transit and at rest (Chapter 6)

7. Protecting against DDoS attacks (Chapter 4)

Unlike the other documents and practices that are available, such as ISO/IEC 27001, the Microsoft OSA does list specific Microsoft technologies that can meet the needs of these specific requirements. When using a cloud platform other that Microsoft Azure, some of these specific features will not be available, and it will be up to the other cloud provider to provide them. If your cloud provider cannot offer sufficient alternatives to the listed Microsoft Azure offerings, a decision needs to be made on behalf of the company.

1. Change to Microsoft Azure

2. Use a multi-cloud solution

Generally speaking, a multi-cloud solution using Microsoft Azure and a second cloud platform becomes complex and potentially performance limiting, as software calls from one cloud to another take time to transfer across the public internet. From a performance perspective alone, a multi-cloud solution isn't often the best practice.

■ **Caution** Having a multi-cloud platform isn't impossible. Several large companies have successfully deployed multi-cloud solutions. However, this is typically done as two different environments, not a single heterogeneous platform. Having a single platform that is spread across multiple cloud platforms, such as Microsoft Azure, Amazon RDS, and Google GCP, is almost always more expensive and more trouble than it is worth. While the concept of multi-cloud is all the rage, it is more expensive than most companies can afford, and more complex than most companies need to deploy.

The big risk that people point to when stating why they want a multi-cloud platform is what if Cloud A goes offline? However, cloud platforms are designed in such a way that an entire cloud platform will never go offline. In each of the three major cloud platforms, each region is an isolated environment unto itself, so even if one region were to go offline the other regions would remain online. Cloud providers have had outages where the management interface was unavailable worldwide for several hours, but the cloud platform itself was still online and available. Virtual machines were online, websites hosted in the platform as a service (PaaS) offering were still available. The only impact was that the management of the services within the cloud wasn't available for a few hours.

While the OSA is vender specific, as it has been released by Microsoft, it can be generalized to be non-Microsoft-specific as the concepts behind the OSA are sound.

The OSA can be found online at https://egits4smb.com/go/osa.

NIST STIG

The United States federal government has published the NIST Risk Management Framework, which is commonly referred to as the NIST STIGs. These documents define background, scoping, and implementation guidance for the security items they cover. In addition, the NIST STIGs provide controls, assessment procedures, and baselines that are needed for the software that the NIST STIG relates to. The NIST STIGs are updated frequently, with the most recent release happening in early 2022, while the prior release was published in September 2020, with updates published in December 2020.

The NIST STIGs must be followed by government computer systems as well as government contractors or suppliers. The NIST frameworks are broken down into the following four categories:

1. Low-Impact
2. Moderate-Impact
3. High-Impact
4. Privacy Control Baseline

How much impact you wish to have on the management of the systems will determine which impact category should be implemented on the system. An example of this can be found in Figure 1-2, where we can see the details for NIST section CM-3, and we can see that no sections of the STIG apply for low-impact systems, two sections apply for moderate-impact systems, and four sections apply to high-impact systems; details for this section can be found at https://egits4smb.com/go/stigcm3.

SP 800-53 Rev 5.1 and SP 800-53B Latest Versions

CM-3 CONFIGURATION CHANGE CONTROL

Family:	CM - CONFIGURATION MANAGEMENT		
Security Baseline:	**Low**	**Moderate**	**High**
	N/A	CM-3 (2) (4)	CM-3 (1) (2) (4) (6)
Privacy Baseline:	N/A		

Figure 1-2. *SP800-53 Revision 5.1 and SP 800-53B*

One of the advantages of the NIST publications is that NIST has data published on just about every commercial software application, from common ones like Microsoft Windows and Microsoft SQL Server, to less common applications such as Sigaba Secure Instance Messaging. These checklists can be found within the National Checklist Program (NCP), which is maintained by NIST and the U.S. federal government.

A full list of the checklists can be found online at `https://egits4smb.com/go/nist-ncp`. The checklists that are published online include all potential vulnerabilities for the software package in question as well as information on how to test to see if your application or server is susceptible to the specific vulnerability. If there is a resolution to the potential issue, that will be listed in the publication as well, which will allow the reader to easily resolve any issues the system is susceptible to.

More information about the NIST Risk Management Framework can be found at `https://egits4smb.com/go/nist`.

PCI DSS

The Payment Card Industry Data Security Standard (PCI DSS) is a standard that should be known by any and every company that handles credit card data. As part of a company's agreements with credit card companies, any systems used in the storing and/or processing of credit card information must fall within the guidelines of the PCI DSS. The determining factor for whether a system falls under the PCI DSS umbrella is if the system stores or processes what the PCI DSS documents refer to as the Primary Account Number (PAN). In non–credit card company speak, this is the credit card number printed on the credit card and stored within the magnetic strip and/or the chip on the credit card. Any systems that handle, process data, or store the PAN are going to be subject to PCI DSS.

At its core the PSI DSS has twelve basic requirements, which are broken down into six sections. These are listed in Table 1-1.

Table 1-1. PCI DSS: High-Level Overview

Section	Requirement
Build and Maintain a Secure Network and Systems	1. Install and maintain a firewall configuration to protect cardholder data.
	2. Do not use vendor-supplied defaults for system passwords and other security parameters.
Protect Cardholder Data	3. Protect stored cardholder data.
	4. Encrypt transmission of cardholder data across open, public networks.
Maintain a Vulnerability Management Program	5. Protect all systems against malware and regularly update anti-virus software or programs.
	6. Develop and maintain secure systems and applications.
Implement Strong Access-Control Measures	7. Restrict access to cardholder data by business need to know.
	8. Identify and authenticate access to system components.
	9. Restrict physical access to cardholder data.
Regularly Monitor and Test Networks	10. Track and monitor all access to network resources and cardholder data.
	11. Regularly test security systems and processes.
Maintain an Information Security Policy	12. Maintain a policy that addresses information security for all personnel.

The full PCI DSS document, which can be downloaded from `https://egits4smb.com/go/pssdss`, contains much more detail about these requirements as well as what information can and cannot be stored in databases and servers that are owned by the company.

While PCI DSS is required for any systems that handle credit cards, following the PCI DSS requirements for any customer-facing systems will provide you with servers and systems that are more secure against both an internal breach as well as an external breach.

The PCI DSS document includes a breakdown of each requirement that is part of the PCI DSS certification, the testing procedures to ensure that the company has fulfilled the requirement, as well as any guidance that the PCI organization has regarding that specific item.

Network Design

The computer network is the core of the infrastructure that facilitates communication between the computers, printers, laptops, and other devices that the company uses. When personal computers were first introduced to the office, the network limited communications to the computers that were physically in the office. As time progressed, these networks connected to the internet, allowing communication with other organizations and the outside world. Today, the computer network has much more than just computers on it. The network at a company today could have security cameras, door locks, badge readers, telephones, call center wall boards, cash registers, printers, scanners, customer computer kiosks, and of course employee computers.

Segmenting networks so that these various devices and their workloads are isolated from each other both improves performance and, most important, protects one network if the other is compromised. The overall goal of this process is to build a series of separate networks that have limited and secured interconnectivity with each other. This process follows the age-old technique of hedging your bets. In network design, we always work under the assumption that part of the network is going to be compromised, and when it is we need to know how the other parts of the network will survive.

One of the most common network design patterns for IT networks is a ringed or segmented network.

© Denny Cherry 2022
D. Cherry, *Enterprise-Grade IT Security for Small and Medium Businesses*,
https://doi.org/10.1007/978-1-4842-8628-9_2

What Is a Ringed Network?

The basic idea behind a ringed network is that it is built looking like a bullseye, with an outer ring, a middle ring, and an inner ring or rings, as shown in Figure 2-1.

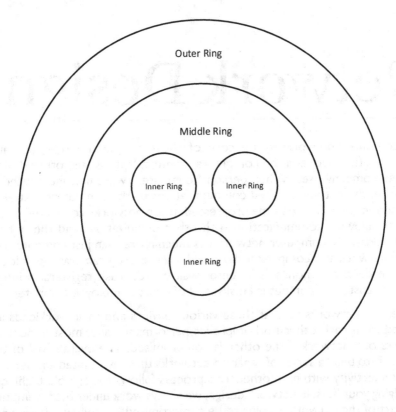

Figure 2-1. Ringed network visualization

The concept behind a ringed network design is that the items that should be the most protected are placed in the inner rings, with no network access from the ring outside that ring unless absolutely needed. For example, the badge readers mentioned in the introduction to this chapter could be placed within an inner ring, with a single opening in the network between the middle ring and the inner ring. An important part of this design is that devices in the outer ring will never be granted access to devices in the inner ring, and devices in the inner rings will never have direct access to devices in the outer ring.

In this network design, the employee computers within the offices would exist within the outer ring, while the servers would exist within the middle ring. To simplify and standardize the terminology, the network rings will be given color codes so that people know which networks others are talking about, similar to the example shown in Figure 2-2.

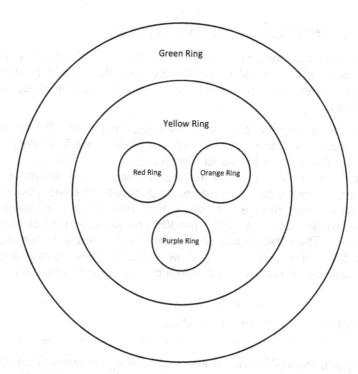

Figure 2-2. Network rings with color names assigned

This ringed approach allows us to have the network isolation that we want and need to properly secure our environment. Because network traffic between the rings isn't allowed unless there is a specific reason, if one ring of the network is compromised the other rings of the network are still secured.

For example, let's put the badge readers and the door locks within the Purple Ring in the preceding example. That network is completely isolated except for a single connection between the building security person's computer and the computer that runs the badge system. In a perfect world, the security person who manages the badge readers would have a second computer that would be connected to the Purple network. That network would be configured so that none of the devices on that network would have internet access. Access to the next ring out, the Yellow ring in this case, would not have access to the network, and none of the sister networks to the Purple network, in this case the Red network and the Orange network, would have access to the Purple network.

This network would effectively be isolated from the rest of the company as well as from the internet. As this network is effectively isolated from everything, and everything is isolated from this network, this network becomes effectively unhackable.

Management of Inner Networks

Having multiple machines isn't always a possibility, as if a person were to manage machines on several different networks, they would need several computers. However, this is the most secure way of handling these sorts of environments.

To support the management of these machines, companies will often turn to a secure access workstation, also known as a SAW. These SAW devices look and function like regular laptop or desktop computers, but are extremely locked down, with the users who use the machines having almost no access to make changes to the devices. Upon bootup these SAW devices will typically connect to a virtual private network (VPN) automatically, with that VPN giving that machine access to only that VPN network, which has extremely limited access. The network that the machine VPNs into will have access to VPN into the Purple network only, allowing that machine to have access to the devices on the Purple network, which then need to be managed.

■ **Note**   We'll discuss VPNs in a later chapter of this book.

In our diagram, the SAW device would be the Orange network. That network would have no access to the internet, and the only access from the internet would be access via the VPN. Since the SAW devices would connect to the VPN network automatically when they booted up, they would effectively be connected to the Orange network as soon as they turned on, often before the user even logged on to the machine. While the VPN connection to the Orange network would be automatic (based on certificates that are installed on the laptop and that cannot be moved to another machine), the VPN connection to the Purple network should be authenticated by a smart card, typically the employee's badge or a secondary employee badge that is only used for this purpose.

These SAW devices have no email client installed, and often have no web browser installed. The user of the machine has no way to install additional software on the machine. This ensures that potential malware would not have the proper permissions to install itself on the device.

For even greater security, after connecting to the Purple network via VPN, the user could be given access to only a jump box via the remote desktop service. This way, the user could remote desktop to the jump box, and from there could remote desktop to the actual machine that is being managed, or the management tools themselves could be installed on that jump box.

Either way, access to the jump box should be extremely limited, with the user's having access to run only the remote desktop client or the management tools that are needed. Like the SAW workstation, no additional software should be installed on this machine, such as an email client or web browser, which could be used as a vector into the jump box.

Separating Customer-Facing Services from Internal Services

Not all servers on the company's computer network are created equal, and they shouldn't be treated as equal either. Any computer that can be accessed from the public internet should be considered as suspect. These machines should be isolated as much as possible from the servers that handle the internal services at the company.

A perfect example is that the servers that run the company's website should be isolated from the computer that runs the firm's internal file server. The internal file server should never be connected to the public internet, just as the public internet has no need to be connecting to the internal server. The servers that are running the company's public-facing website can't be trusted, as unknown users could connect to them.

Because of this we want to isolate the publicly accessible servers from the internal servers. Ideally, we want a full block of access between these servers, but in most cases that isn't totally possible, so we need to be content with having almost a complete lockdown between these internet-facing servers and anything that is internal that they need access to. Those computers that can be accessed from the internet are placed in a "demilitarized zone," or DMZ.

Note   Yes, we use the same name as the DMZ that exists between North and South Korea.

By default, this DMZ network is totally isolated from the internal network, with no connectivity between them. If connectivity is needed, for example between a web server and the database server that provides the information needed by the website, then a single hole is opened in the firewall that blocks the access. This single hole grants access from the web servers' machines to the database server using the network port needed by the database server. In the case of Microsoft SQL Server, this access would be over port 1433. In the case of Oracle, this access would be over port 1521. In the case of MySQL, this access would be over port 3306. While different databases have different port numbers, they will all require a tiny bit of access between the front-end machines and the database servers.

Note   Firewalls will be discussed in Chapter 3 of this book.

The public internet should not have unfettered access to the machines in the DMZ. These public machines should have a firewall between the public internet and the machines, which will ensure that only the network ports that are needed are opened. The DMZ should contain only web servers, and the only network ports that would typically need to be opened are ports 80 and 443. Port 80 is used for unencrypted website traffic using the Hypertext Transfer Protocol (HTTP), while port 443 is used for secure website traffic using the Hypertext Transfer Protocol Secure (HTTPS). Unless there is a need for other access from the internet to the machines in the DMZ, there should be no other access by default.

Much like the connections between the internet and the DMZ, access between the DMZ and the internal network should be secured by default with just the minimum access possible going between the networks. In the most secure environments, there will be no access from the internal servers to the DMZ. This prevents users from accessing the computers on the DMZ unless they have an approved way to manage these machines.

Oftentimes, companies will have what is referred to as a jump box. The administrator connects to the jump box, and then from the jump box they have access to the servers in the DMZ. This way, the machines within the DMZ are secured, while still allowing the system administration team to manage the computers. Typically access to the jump box will be limited to the remote desktop service when using Windows, or to the secure shell (SSH) protocol in a Unix or Linux environment.

■ **Tip** Often when doing deployments within Microsoft Azure customers ask for these DMZ machines to be inaccessible from the internet network. This makes the management of these machines challenging. However, Microsoft Azure has a service called Azure Bastion, which is effectively a jump box as a service, which allows for connection to these machines via remote desktop for Microsoft Windows computers, or the SSH command-line tool for Linux computers, all via a web browser. This prevents us from needing a direct connection to the computers in the DMZ from the internal network while providing an additional layer of authentication before allowing access to the computers within the DMZ, as using the Azure Bastion service requires first authenticating to the Azure portal, which can be configured for features such as multi-factor authentication (which will be discussed in Chapter 6 of this book).

By isolating the computers in the DMZ from the computers on the internal network and isolating the computers on the internal network from the computers on the DMZ, we protect these computers from each other and, most important, from the end users who work on computers within the company. This isolation provides a safety net, keeping a virus infection or ransomware infection from spreading from one network of machines to another.

While isolating servers from each other may seem like overkill, it very much isn't. Network attacks happen against internet-connected servers all day and all night, with the bad actors who control such attacks running them from all around the world at all hours. Even if a company were to spot a successful network attack in real time, by the time the company were able to respond by turning off the internet access of the machines in question, it would be too late.

Some services are going to need to be a bridge between these environments. These are typically database servers that need the ability to have production data on them, but still need to allow company employees to have some sort of access in order to perform activities, such as running reports or ad-hoc SQL statements against the servers. In these cases, the best practice would be for the users to remote desktop into a jump box, which they can then use to query the reporting SQL server. Production customer data should never be copied from the production network to an internal location where the end users can have direct access to the database server, even when that database server is hosting just a copy of the production data.

We must work under the assumption that there are always going to be attacks in progress, and we need to configure our equipment such that we always assume that an attack has been successful.

One of the reasons that we isolate users from internal servers, and internal servers from DMZ servers, is that the most common cause of a successful ransomware attack is an end user. Those end users are most often unwitting participants in the attack. We need to ensure that when the user's computer is breached, making them an unwitting participant, the servers that run the company are protected. If our security posture is set up correctly and users are sufficiently isolated from the servers, and if a ransomware infection completely encrypts the hard drives of every desktop computer in the company, not a single server will be infected.

If the servers are safe, the company can continue to function while its information is completely safe, while the users' desktop computers are all formatted and reinstalled.

The end goal of security is to make all the computers on the network safe and protected, but in reality the servers and the workstations (either desktops or laptops) are two different classes of computers, and they should be treated as such, with the servers protected from the workstations. This doesn't mean that we can place the workstations on the public internet with no protection, but as these are the computers on which users receive email and surf the internet, these machines need to be isolated from the servers that run the company, as the servers need to be able to function even if every workstation is compromised.

Isolation of Workloads

One of the goals of network design is to ensure the isolation of workloads so that they cannot have access to machines and processes to which they do not need access. A core tenet of IT security in general is that you don't need access to what you don't need to do your work. This principal is called the principal of least privilege. Taking this to the extreme is really what needs to be done given the current state of the internet and how easy it is to attempt to break into a company's information technology environment.

We want to apply this isolation to people as well as computers by only giving employees access to what they need in order to complete their assigned tasks—no more access, and no less.

By giving a person more access to systems than they need to complete their job, we open up those systems to the risk of being compromised by a bad actor who gets access to the employee's credentials. While it is easier and faster to give a person access to more than they need, this opens up more risk. In information technology, the end goal is to eliminate risk, or when the risk can't be eliminated to reduce it as much as possible and mitigate the residual risk so that the risk is at an acceptable level, and the remaining risk is known, documented, and understood by everyone.

Part of isolation involves things like network design and the placement of jump boxes to ensure that the systems can be managed while being isolated from each other. The other part of isolation involves training employees that shortcuts around the isolation shouldn't be taken, and that if there are shortcuts around the isolation found, those shouldn't be used by the employees but instead reported to IT management so that the issue can be categorized and the workaround blocked as needed.

One of the concerns with Windows jump boxes is that you can copy and paste files or text through the remote desktop service. This functionality can and should be disabled on jump boxes so that files and text cannot be copied through the jump box. While this does make deployments of software harder, it helps secure the jump box and the production environment from unknown applications' being copied onto it, and it also prevents data from being copied out of the production environment via the jump box.

Examples of this isolation can be found at companies that completely isolate their customer-facing production environment from both the internet and internal users. At its most extreme, this requires dedicated machines that are the only way to access these environments, and even in these cases a jump box is required in order to better secure the production environment.

For example, let's say that we work for the company Contoso, and our staff logs in to their work computers using their email address, username@ contoso.com. The system administration team that manages the production servers would have dedicated laptops that are configured to VPN into the edge of the production network. From there, the administrator could remote desktop to a jump box, from which they could access the production servers. When the administrator logs in to the production servers, they should not be using the same account they use to log in to their desktop and to check their email. Some companies will set up administrative accounts, with either an "a-" before the username, an "-a" after the username, or a totally different username altogether. Some companies will go to the extreme and have a totally different Active Directory environment set up in order to fully isolate the production environment, requiring the administrators to sign in to the production servers as username@contoso.prod.

No matter which patten is used, the important part is that the administrators shouldn't be logging in to the production environment with the same account they use to log in to their desktop machines and to check email, sign in to the company chat application, etc.

The reason for this separation is risk mitigation. In the event that the administrator's username and password are compromised, and a bad actor is able to get into the network, it won't help any as those credentials aren't used to log in to the production servers.

We've now taken the risk associated with needing access to both an email address and the production servers and mitigated it by having a different account be used for each. Having the production servers on a separate Active Directory domain has an advantage here, in that if the machines are part of the same Active Directory domain as the desktop computer, there's a risk of an attacker's elevating their permissions though known, but not yet patched, exploits and gaining access to the production servers. By placing those servers in the contoso.prod Active Directory domain, and keeping the contoso.prod and contoso.com Active Directory domains separate from each other, we have again mitigated this risk.

We can further mitigate this risk by requiring that, to sign in to the jump box, a proxy card be inserted into the desktop computer. To successfully log in to the jump box, the person needs to have the proxy card. The proxy card contains a certificate that is issued to only the proxy card, and if it were duplicated it wouldn't match the certificate and would then not be validated.

While this does create additional steps for the administrator, it produces a more secure environment. When it comes to information technology workers, the goal should be to create a safe and secure environment, with the security of the environment as the top concern. All too often the top concern of administrators will be finding how to manage the environment quickly and easily. The short answer is you don't. As the person with the responsibility of designing a secure environment, I'm not that concerned with the fact that the administration team is going to have to jump through a few hoops in order to manage the environment.

▓ **Note**   Several years ago, I was working with a team and they told me that it was going to be hard to manage the system as it was designed, because they didn't want to use jump boxes and they wanted to be able to copy and paste files between the servers and their workstations.

They were not fans of the response they got. My response was basically "too bad." Their job was to manage the environment and have the environment be safe and secure. The fact that they couldn't do things the way they had always done things wasn't the point of the security exercise.

No matter which approach is taken to have separate accounts for general work and administrative tasks, having separate accounts is the key to having a secure environment.

Separation of Duties

Separation of duties requires having different members of the company's staff performing different roles. In this process, individual staff members handle individual tasks, without crossing into the tasks that are handled by other members of the company.

The separation of duties generally requires an increased number of employees, as the employees can only handle individual tasks. Because of the increased number of employees, this process can often be outside the reach of small and medium businesses.

An example of the separation of duties would be the operation of the servers that run the company. The management of the server would be split into several different categories, such as general operating system management, network configuration, and security (and permissions), with each of these three categories falling under the purview of a separate member of the IT team.

By separating duties among different members of the organization, we can minimize the damage done by any one person or bad actor who gains access to an employee's credentials. While this does potentially increase the number of employees that a company needs, the risk to the organization resulting from not separating duties can be massive.

Separation of duties can be taken to the extreme with different employees managing the development and production environments. While this might seem to be extreme, this level of separation can help the company protect itself in the event that one of the employees becomes disgruntled against the company, or if the employee's account is compromised. The end result is that no single administrator has access to the entire company environment, so if the employee's account is used to do damage to company resources, it can only be used to damage a part of the company's environment.

The end goal of all these various techniques is to protect the company and minimize the attack surface area in the event that the company is attacked, either from the inside or from the outside. The reality is that approximately 66 *percent* of data breaches that impact companies are performed by employees. This means that when we design our networks and policies, we need to account for the fact that an employee will more than likely attempt to leak company data, and protect against this eventuality.

Firewalls

A firewall is a hardware appliance or software package that is designed to prevent users from accessing a computer, network, or endpoint. Just like their physical namesake in a car or a building, where the firewall exists to stop fire and/or heat from moving from one place to another, a computer firewall is designed to stop data from moving from one place to another.

What Do Firewalls Do?

The primary responsibility of a firewall is to stop network traffic that is coming from one network to access the other network. As we can see from the high-level network diagram shown in Figure 3-1, the firewall sits between networks, preventing the internet network traffic from accessing the network traffic of the devices on the private network.

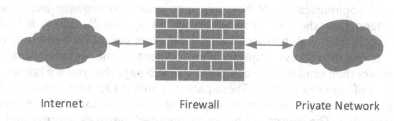

Internet   Firewall   Private Network

Figure 3-1. High-level network diagram

D. Cherry, *Enterprise-Grade IT Security for Small and Medium Businesses*,
https://doi.org/10.1007/978-1-4842-8628-9_3

Firewalls function through a series of rules that tell the firewall what network traffic to let through the device. Modern firewalls will do more than just allow network traffic through them or not. Most modern firewalls also perform a process called network address translation (NAT). This NAT process serves two goals. It is used to mask the actual IP addresses of computers on the internal network from the internet, and it also allows companies to use what are called private IP address ranges.

Public IP addresses are what we call fully routable addresses. This means that the internet knows how to route network traffic to these IP addresses, and knows what networks are connected to what networks, so that my computer knows how to access public websites, such as www.amazon.com.

However, we don't want to assign every computer at our company a public IP address as this would increase the speed at which the world will run out of IP addresses. The IP address range which is typically used is called IPv4 and contains only ~4.2 billion IP addresses. If every internet connected device needed a public IP address the list of available IP addresses would have long run out. In order to prevent this we use NAT combined with private IP addresses at companies which are non-internet routable.

When we say that the private IP addresses are not routable, we don't mean that devices that have these IP addresses can't access the internet. It means that they can't directly access the internet without using a firewall (or device or router) that supports NAT. If we took a computer that had a private IP address and connected that computer directly to the internet, the internet wouldn't know how to route our traffic out to the internet, or back to our computer from the internet. By using NAT, we can have computers with private IP addresses, and have those computers access the internet.

When computers talk to each other, they use network packets to perform the actual communication. When you open your web browser and type in www.amazon.com, the web browser first looks up the IP address for www.amazon.com. The web browser sends a network packet to Amazon's web server, at that IP address, requesting the content of the website. Amazon's web servers then send to your computer the web page that you are requesting as a series of network packets. These packets contain a lot of information, but the information they contain that's important to this discussion is the source and destination. The source will be your computer's network address, and the destination will be Amazon's web server.

When we use NAT between our computers and the public internet either the source or the destination address will be changed. Within NAT we have two flavors, called Source Network Address Translation (SNAT) and Destination Network Address Translation (DNAT). These protocols are what will change the packet header in the request.

SNAT

With SNAT, the source of the request is changed. In our example of accessing Amazon's website, the SNAT process will change the source IP address of the packet from the private IP address of our computer to the public IP address of the firewall. This way, when the Amazon website replies with the network packets, it will put the public IP address of the firewall. As the packet is a response to your request, SNAT will take the network packet from Amazon and replace that network address with the network address of your computer. SNAT is specially designed for allowing computers at the company to access the public internet.

In the diagram in Figure 3-2 we can see this in play. Our computer on the internal network has received a network address of 10.0.0.3, and our firewall has the public IP address of 207.212.72.12.

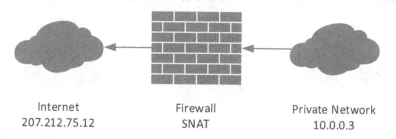

Internet	Firewall	Private Network
207.212.75.12	SNAT	10.0.0.3

Figure 3-2. SNAT network topology

When we access a web page from our computer, the network packets have a source address of 10.0.0.3. That IP address won't work on the public internet, as lots of companies and home networks use the same private IP space. When the SNAT process works, it takes the network packet and replaces 10.0.0.3 with the firewall's public IP address of 207.212.75.12. This then allows the web server to respond, and it is responding to the firewall. The SNAT process knows that the packets are actually for your computer, so it changes the packet address back from its public IP address to 10.0.0.3 so that the packets can make their way to your computer and then be shown in your web browser.

DNAT

With DNAT, the destination address within the packet is changed. Unlike SNAT, DNAT is designed to allow computers on the public internet to access devices on your private network. While technically these could be any kind of device, in most cases these will be web servers.

While SNAT is designed to replace the source IP address, DNAT is designed to replace the destination IP address. This allows computers on the public internet to access web servers that are protected by a firewall. One of the benefits of DNAT is that the web servers don't need public IP addresses. Giving web servers public IP address would cause a couple of problems, the first being that this increased number of needed IP addresses would increase the speed at which IPv4 addresses will run out. The second benefit is that this increases the chances that unwanted processes will be exposed to the public internet, making it easier for a bad actor to access the server.

When a user goes to a website that is protected by a firewall via DNAT, the user's network packet hits the firewall, and the firewall changes the destination address on the packet from the public IP address of the DNAT rule to the private IP address that is entered in the firewall rule. We can see this in Figure 3-3 where our DNAT rule has a public IP address of 207.212.75.17 and our web server has a private IP address of 10.0.0.21.

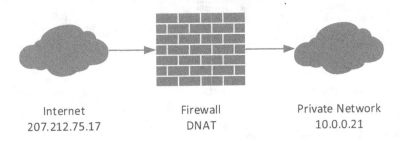

| Internet | Firewall | Private Network |
| 207.212.75.17 | DNAT | 10.0.0.21 |

Figure 3-3. DNAT network topology

As users request to get pages from our web server, those request are sent to the front end of the firewall, which is listening on the IP address 207.212.75.17. When that request is processed by the DNAT service on the firewall, the IP address that is shown as the destination of the packet is changed to 10.0.0.21. This allows the packet to be sent to the web server, which can then respond with the web page that the user wanted to see.

DNAT is important from a security perspective as we don't want to put public IP addresses on our servers; DNAT allows for this. As we can see in Figure 3-3, the server does not have the public IP address configured on it. If the server had the public IP address entered on it, then all services installed on the computer would be available on that server's public IP address by default. If the web server were a server with the Windows operating system installed on it, those services would include the Remote Desktop Service, the file-sharing service, and any other services that are installed on the web server that we don't want exposed to the public internet. Instead of putting the public IP address directly on the web server, the DNAT service hosts the public IP address, and the responses are handled by the firewall itself.

Does My Company Need a Firewall?

The short answer is yes. There is going to be a longer answer, which will also boil down to yes.

Most companies are not just a single office. For the purposes of this section, we're going to assume we have a company that has an office with employees and a few internal servers, a colocation facility that hosts some other servers, and a cloud environment that is hosted in Microsoft Azure.

The Office

No matter how big or small an office you have, there should be some sort of firewall device that sits between the network router and the public internet. If your office has cable internet from the local cable company, then the firewall may need to sit inside of the cable modem. No matter where it is, there should be a firewall of some sort. A huge number of companies sell firewall appliances at a variety of price points. The larger the office, the more expensive a firewall is going to be needed.

Remember that this firewall is going to be the primary protection for the network from the internet for the company at this office. That probably means that all of your customer data, sales data, etc. is stored on servers at the office. Your customers won't want their contact information leaked on the public internet. A firewall is going to be important to ensure that everything is safe.

This becomes even more important in smaller companies. Smaller companies will often get consumer-grade internet at their office as the speed is good enough, the cost is reasonable, and the service-level guarantee is good enough. The problem comes down to the equipment that is provided. Consumer-grade cable modems are set with a default username and password that's controlled by the cable company. Those default usernames are usually statically set by the provider, and well documented on the internet. This means that once an attacker figures out what kind of cable modem you have installed, it's pretty easy for them to search for the default username and password for that device and then configure it to let them connect to the inside network.

This is why a firewall is so important.

Figure 3-4 shows the ideal small office setup. This may not always be possible and will largely depend on what kind of physical network connection is provided by the internet service provider and how many public IP addresses they provide you.

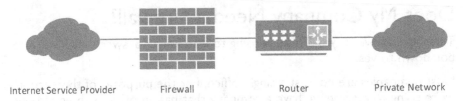

Internet Service Provider   Firewall   Router   Private Network

Figure 3-4. Preferred small office network configuration

In Figure 3-4, we can see that the ISP connects directly to the firewall. In order to have a configuration like this, the ISP will need to provide an Ethernet cable as the termination of their cable. If the internet is provided by the cable TV company they may not be able to do this, as the internet comes in via a coaxial line or a fiber optic line, through which the cable TV service is delivered.

From the firewall, there's a network cable to the router, and from there to all the devices on the internet network.

Many small-office routers have a firewall built into them, so having just a single device is possible just so long as all the router's management functions are blocked from the public internet.

In the event that you have internet being delivered to the office (or a home office, for that matter), you probably will not be able to put a firewall in front of the router that's provided by the internet service provider. In this case, the firewall will need to be on the inner side of the network from the router, as shown in Figure 3-5.

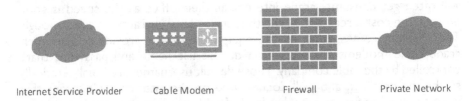

Internet Service Provider   Cable Modem   Firewall   Private Network

Figure 3-5. Small office network configuration for cable modems

What usually happens in this sort of configuration is that the firewall is actually doing routing (and NAT) as well as being a firewall. What we end up having in these situations is a double NAT system. This is because the cable modem does basic routing, and we need the important routing to be done by the firewall. This is shown in Figure 3-6.

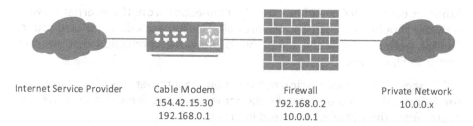

Internet Service Provider   Cable Modem   Firewall   Private Network
                            154.42.15.30   192.168.0.2   10.0.0.x
                            192.168.0.1   10.0.0.1

Figure 3-6. Network configuration for cable modems

As we can see in Figure 3-6, the cable modem gets a public IP address from the internet service provider, 154.42.15.30 in this case. The cable modem has a private IP address of 192.168.0.1. As we can't trust the network that the cable modem is providing, we connect our firewall to the inside of the cable modem. On the public side of the firewall, we use an IP address of 192.168.0.2 so that the "public" side of the firewall can talk to our cable modem. On the inside of the firewall, we use the IP address of 10.0.0.1, and then all of the devices on the inside of the office get IP addresses from the same 10.0.0.x network.

This sort of dual NAT configuration works because everything to the right of the firewall in Figure 3-5 is our trusted internet network. Everything to the left of our firewall is untrusted, including the cable modem from the internet service provider.

It is important to never expect the ISP to provide any sort of firewall services unless they are specifically contracted to. Unless there is something in writing that says that the provider will provide a service, don't expect them to do so. And even if they will, based on your contract, assume that they won't, and be happy if they actually do. It's better than being disappointed if they don't, when you expect them to provide it. Remember, you only get one chance to stop a breach.

The Colocation Facility

Colocation facilities are used to host servers for companies. These facilities are typically built where there are internet links from several different internet providers, and cheap, reliable power is provided by at least one provider. Often, colocation facilities will have power from at least two power grids.

The networking at all colocation facilities is more consistent than that in small offices. This is because computer networking and hosting is their business, so they make it easy to connect to their networks. The network connection from the ISP at a colocation facility will pretty much always be either a fiber optic connection or an Ethernet connection. Enterprise firewalls will have network ports in them that can hold either fiber channel connectors or

Ethernet connectors. In either case, the connection from the internet service provider should terminate into the firewall. This network design should sound familiar, because this is the same sort of network connection that we saw earlier in Figure 3-4.

While there will be more logical networks on the internet side of the network, the front end should be basically the same, with the firewall protecting the router from the outside, untrusted internet.

Firewalls and the Cloud

When it comes to the cloud, we don't have the option of having a physical device in front of our services. However, there are still firewall options available to us in the cloud. The big difference between cloud firewall options and physical firewalls is that in the cloud the firewalls are all software based, instead of physical appliances. This doesn't make these appliances any less robust.

■ **Note**   As you'll notice from continuing to read through this section, all the cloud providers are in a race to come up with the dumbest names possible for their network services.

Microsoft Azure

Microsoft Azure has a very robust firewall ecosystem. You can choose the Microsoft Azure Firewall service, which is a Platform as a Service (PaaS) offering. Because it is a PaaS offering, there is no maintenance to be done of the virtual machines hosting the firewall. You simply configure the Azure Firewall service (including DNAT), and it handles everything else.Microsoft has provided Azure Firewall Manager to simplify the managing of firewall rules for the Azure Firewall service. With Azure Firewall Manager, you can create nested policies, allowing for a common set of rules that are shared among all deployed Azure Firewalls, while allowing each Azure Firewall to have configurations specific to that Azure Firewall device.

Within Microsoft Azure, there are two components that need to be configured. There's the Azure Firewall, which is the actual firewall service, and there is the Firewall Policy, which is configured through Azure Firewall Manager. Microsoft has separated these configurations from each other so that a policy can be set once and then applied to multiple firewalls.

Within the Azure Firewall policy you can configure DNAT rules, network rules, and application rules.

DNAT rules specify how internet users will be accessing internal services, such as internet-facing web servers.

Network rules are designed to allow outbound access from the virtual machines to the internet. By default, when Azure Firewall is deployed, the virtual machines protected by Azure Firewall do not have access to the internet, unless a network rule has been put in place to allow this access.

Application rules are like network rules in that they define outbound connectivity options. Network rules allow you to specify a network protocol and a port number or series of port numbers to open, while an application rule allows you to specify a protocol name to open. Where a network rule would specify "TCP port 80," an application rule would specify "http."

Microsoft Azure allows you to use a variety of third-party firewalls as well as the native Azure Firewall service. Third-party firewalls are firewall solutions made available by the companies that produce the hardware version of the firewall. These third-party firewall solutions are most often chosen by companies when those companies have on-staff expertise in that platform.

If your company has staff expertise in Cisco firewalls, using the Microsoft Azure Firewall service wouldn't make the most of your staff's experience. Thankfully, Microsoft has virtual Cisco firewalls as an option, allowing you to deploy the virtual Cisco firewall, thus giving the administrators of the firewall the same experience in managing the firewall as they would have normally.

There are third-party firewalls available from basically every physical firewall vendor, including F5, Cisco, Fortinet, Barracuda, etc.

Whether an Azure firewall or a third-party firewall, the network design is very similar. The chosen firewall appliance hosts the public IP addresses. The firewall then does the NAT and connects the internet user with the internet resource they are attempting to access, as shown in Figure 3-7.

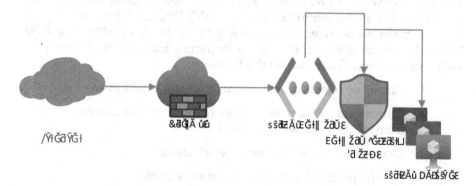

Figure 3-7. Microsoft Azure network design

As you can see, the Azure firewall (or third-party firewall) sits between the internet and the virtual machines. All network traffic to and from the virtual machines passes through the Azure Firewall service, protecting the machines from the internet.

In addition to the Azure Firewall platform, Microsoft Azure also includes a web application firewall (WAF). A WAF is designed to protect a website from attack vectors, such as SQL injection, cross-site scripting, and brute-force and botnet attacks, while the Azure Firewall service is designed to block network traffic from entering or exiting the Azure virtual network. Many websites will have a WAF deployed as well as the Azure Firewall service, as these features do two different things while having very similar names.

Configuration of the Azure Firewall service can be completed in a variety of methods, including ARM templates, Microsoft PowerShell, Azure command-line interface (CLI), or the Microsoft Azure portal. This gives a variety of options for configuring the system and, if needed, checking the scripts required to change the firewall configuration to a source control system.

Amazon Web Services (AWS)

Amazon's AWS cloud platform has a robust firewall solution ecosystem. AWS provides their AWS Firewall Manager, which allows you to create and manage your firewall rules on a variety of AWS services, including the AWS web application firewall (WAF), AWS Shield Advanced protections, AWS Network Firewall rules, as well as AWS Route 53.

The AWS Network Firewall is the AWS managed service that provides protection for Amazon Virtual Private Clouds (VPCs). This service allows for the creation of firewall rules to allow both inbound and outbound connections to be blocked or allowed as needed.

The AWS Network Firewall allows you to filter your inbound and outbound network traffic at the perimeter of your AWS VPC platform, enabling the network traffic to be rejected before it gets to the AWS VMs. The AWS Network Firewall allows traffic to be inspected and identified through a variety of methods. These include the following:

1. Passing or rejecting traffic through known IP addresses

2. Custom lists of domain names to prevent applications from reaching known bad domains

3. Deep packet inspection on network traffic

4. Stateful protocol detection on network traffic

Configuration of the AWS Network Firewall can be completed in a variety of ways, including the AWS portal, AWS command-line interface (CLI), AWS tools for Windows PowerShell, or the AWS Network Firewall application programming interface (API). This gives a variety of options for configuring the system and, if needed, checking the scripts needed to change the firewall configuration to a source control system.

Google Cloud Platform (GCP)

GCP provides a robust firewall solution. The Google firewall is always enabled and blocks or allows network traffic to and from the virtual machines hosted within your GCP environment. These firewall rules allow you to specify both the inbound and the outbound rules, based on the remote IP address range.

By default, the Google GCP firewall will have a number of default rules already applied when the firewall is first activated. These rules will ensure that the virtual machines that are protected by the Google GCP firewall are able to talk to the firewall service. There is also a default rule that blocks all access from the internet to the virtual machines, but allows traffic from the virtual machines to the internet. This default rule, which allows the virtual machines to connect to websites on the internet, can (and should) be overwritten by a rule that denies access to the internet.

Non-Major Cloud Providers

There are a variety of cloud providers beyond the big three (Microsoft Azure, Amazon AWS, and Google GCP). Those providers may or may not have a firewall service like the big three providers do. If the provider being used doesn't have a firewall service and they expect you to provide and configure a firewall solution within their platform, then it may be time to consider a migration to a different cloud service.

Access to the Internet

When hosting services in the cloud, regardless of the provider being used, those machines and services do not need access to the internet by default. One very important step in securing your cloud platform is to ensure that the virtual machines within the cloud platform have very limited access to the internet. This means that all outbound connections should be blocked, unless they are specifically allowed.

By default, only a few connections should be allowed, as follows:

1. DNS requests
2. Windows updates
3. Deployment repositories

DNS requests are going to need to be allowed to order to make the other connections function. Without DNS, the servers within the cloud platform aren't going to be able to connect to anything else.

Windows updates are going to be needed for any machines that are running a Microsoft Windows operating system. The easiest way to allow this access is to allow all the machines to use the public internet Windows Update servers. However some companies may not allow this. For those companies, you can use the Microsoft WSUS service, or a third-party patching software platform. This software is installed on a server within your cloud infrastructure, and that machine has the ability to contact the Windows Update servers on the internet. This machine will then download all of the patches for whatever Microsoft (or third-party) software products and make those patches available. All of the other machines within your environment can be configured to use that server to download the patches. This reduces the number of machines that will need access to any part of the internet.

Machines running Linux (or Unix) platforms will need access to their deployment repositories. These deployment repositories are where published software has been deployed so that it is easier for the administrator of the system to download and install the needed software packages. Updates for the software packages are also deployed to these deployment repositories. To install and patch the software needed for the cloud computers, access to these repositories by the machines is needed.

Firewalls Aren't Just for the Cloud

Firewalls aren't just for servers in the cloud. Offices and colocation facilities should also have firewalls configured. The big difference between cloud and on-premises firewalls is that the cloud firewalls will be software based while the on-premises firewalls will typically be physical devices. The configuration is basically the same whether the device is a virtual device or a physical device. Weather using a physical or virtual firewall, the firewall will have rules that allow or deny network traffic, and by default all internet access should be blocked.

With offices, blocking internet access becomes harder. Employees need internet access to do their jobs. This presents a challenge for configuring firewall rules, as access to the internet needs to be enabled, but network traffic needs to be inspected by the firewall or other devices to ensure that the network traffic isn't malicious.

Use a Firewall

Unless a machine needs internet access to reach out to a specific internet website, to contact a partner/vendor/customer/etc., that internet access should be blocked. We want to block all internet access by default to prevent any virus, ransomware, or other hacking software from phoning home to get instructions. By blocking outbound internet access, we can prevent most data exfiltration events. This gives us an extra layer of protection in that even if someone were able to get into the network with the goal of stealing large amounts of data, they wouldn't be able to push those files out to an internet server. This is especially true for ransomware attacks. These attacks are typically automated and require the ability for the ransomware software to connect to the command-and-control server on the internet. By blocking this access, the ransomware software won't have a way to check in with the people who wrote and control the software. This will prevent the software from checking in and telling the writers that the software has been installed, and that it is ready to encrypt the machines.

Distributed Denial of Service

A denial of service attack against a computer network, is a network based attack with the goal of taking the network offline. This can prevent the company users from being able to access the internet as well as preventing external customers from accessing resources such as the companies website.

Many people think that a Denial of Service attack can be resolved by having a traditional Firewall in place. This is not the case, as a Denial of Service attack requires specific hardware in order to mitigate the attack.

What Is a Denial-of-Service Attack?

A denial-of-service attack is a network attack in which the person who is committing the attack is attempting to flood the network of the company they are attacking. This attack works by sending a mass of traffic from the source network to the target network. The network traffic sent as part of a denial-of-service attack is random, generic data that can be discarded. While the data is garbage data, it appears legitimate enough that the network devices accept the data and attempt to process it.

The result of a denial-of-service attack is that the victim's network connection is filled with network traffic, and the router that received the traffic becomes overloaded attempting to process the inbound stream of data. This causes the

© Denny Cherry 2022
D. Cherry, *Enterprise-Grade IT Security for Small and Medium Businesses*,
https://doi.org/10.1007/978-1-4842-8628-9_4

target of the attack to lose internet access for the period of the attack, possibly longer, as the overloaded router might need to be restarted.

A device that protects the network from a denial-of-service attack is designed to look at the network traffic coming into the network from the internet. These devices, after reviewing the network traffic, allow the valid traffic through while disregarding the traffic from a denial-of-service attack.

Denial-of-service attacks are the most successful when the attack lasts for days or weeks. This means that the network that is suffering a denial-of-service attack will be offline for the duration of the attack, potentially for weeks. An attack that is perpetrated against an office network will prevent any employees at the office from being able to access the internet. An attack perpetrated against a Colocation facility will prevent any internet-facing services, such as websites, FTP servers, etc., from working. Internet users who attempt to access websites hosted on these networks will receive errors showing that the websites are unresponsive and offline. These network connections will be unavailable for the duration of the denial-of-service attack, leading to customers' not being able to access websites for potentially weeks. This can lead to lost revenue as customers aren't able to access the company's websites or purchase the company's products.

When a company's office network is attacked and employees aren't able to access the internet from the office, the employees are not able to complete their work. If the employees are processing customer orders and need to access an internet-hosted website in order to do so, they will not be able to as the office network will be completely flooded with internet traffic.

Denial-of-service attacks are different from ransomware attacks. With denial-of-service attacks there's no way to identify the group that is attacking the network. While the individual IP addresses that are the cause of the attack are trackable and blockable, the people behind the attack won't be identifiable. As there is no way to identify the attackers, there is no way to stop the attack. This means that the only way to stop the attack is to simply wait for the person or group that is perpetrating the attack to get bored and stop.

Denial-of-service attacks have been around for decades, and they are only increasing in frequency and duration.

What Is a Distributed Denial of Service Attack?

A distributed denial of service (DDoS) attack is similar to a denial-of-service attack. The big difference between the two is that with a distributed denial of service attack, the source of the attack is scaled from one computer or network to a large number of remote computers on different networks. This allows the attacker to send an even greater amount of garbage network traffic to the target network.

This amplifies the results of the attack. These attacks are typically run by botnets, meaning that the people whose computers are being used to perpetrate the attack are unaware that their computers are being used in the attack. These distributed attacks can involve thousands or even tens of thousands of computers.

There are two different types of DDoS attack, depending on the goal of the attack. The first is a bits-per-second attack, while the second is a packets-per-second attack. With a bits-per-second attack, the goal is to overload the network link to the company. With a packets-per-second attack, the goal is to overload the network equipment at the target site.

The amount of network traffic being generated in these attacks is massive.

A recent Distributed Denial of Service attack against a large European bank clocked in at 809 million packets per second, more than double the previous record on the Akamai platform.

— Fred Donovan, `https://egits4smb.com/go/ddos`

When performing a packets-per-second attack, such as the attack in the preceding quote, the network packets that are sent contain just the packet header so that the routers need to process them. This allows the attackers to send more packets through the network connection, which forces the CPU of the target router to process more packets per second. When the number of network packets that are sent to a router increases, the CPU of the router works harder in order to process those requests.

When performing a bits-per-second attack, such as an attack against the Amazon Web Services (AWS) infrastructure in 2020, which was recorded at 2.3 terabits per second, the goal of the attack is to overload the network connection the website is hosted on. This attack was 44 percent larger than the prior largest attack against AWS.

With a bits-per-second attack, there are several different variants that could be used. With the preceding AWS attack, the attack was done via forged packets, where requests were sent to a Lightweight Directory Access Protocol (LDAP) hosted on the internet. In this attack, the requests to the LDAP server were sent with the source IP address being the AWS infrastructure instead of the attacking machine(s).

In another attack, this time in 2020 against Akamai, which is a global network security and content delivery company, there were a variety of attack vectors. This attack peaked at 1.44 terabits per second.

Nine different vectors were used, so they were really throwing the kitchen sink, trying to find the chink in the armor to create some damage for this particular customer along the way.

— Roger Barranco, VP of Global Security Operations, Akamai

Distributed denial of service attacks don't need to attack your services to be successful. This is evident while reviewing an attack against Dyn DNS, which happened in 2016 and is considered to be one of the most successful distributed denial of service attacks. This attack took down their DNS service, which hosts the DNS records for a variety of companies, including Twitter, SoundCloud, PayPal, Etsy, Reddit, PlayStation, and others. More details about this distributed denial of service attack can be found at https://egits4smb.com/go/dyndns.

Why Are Distributed Denial of Service Attacks Done?

The short answer to why distributed denial of service attacks are done is simply because they can be done. The longer answer depends on why the company or organization is being attacked.

The person launching the attack often has some sort of personal grudge against the company that is being attacked. The attack could be run by a former employee or a disgruntled customer (or former customer), or could be completely random, with the attacker's having no connection to the company at all.

During the Russian invasion of Ukraine in 2022, the hacker collective Anonymous said that they hacked into a variety of Russian state assets, including the state-backed news agency Russia Today (RT), which suffered a distributed denial of service attack against their infrastructure.

In the past, DDoS attacks against companies have occurred when attackers wanted to cause havoc with former employers or companies from which they have purchased items. DDoS attacks can be just as damaging to a company as a threat against the physical office, such as a bomb theat. While a phoned-in bomb threat will affect a company for a few hours while the building is evacuated and searched, a distributed denial of service attack can take the internet connection for the company offline for days or weeks. Basically, as long as the attacker wants (or until the company has installed an appliance to block the DDoS attack), the attack will continue.

When these distributed denial of service attacks happen, the attacker doesn't typically contact the company looking for some reason to stop the attack. The attack simply continues until the attacker is bored with the attack. These attacks are successful due to the fact that they are anonymous. There is no way to track back who started a distributed denial of service attack. If the company that is being attacked were to monitor the network traffic that is attacking them, the network traffic would come from hundreds, or thousands, or even tens of thousands of computers, none of which will belong to the actual attackers. The machines attacking will have one or more viruses installed on them, with those machines checking in to a command-and-control server that gives them their instructions.

Distributed Denial of Service Attacks as a Service

In the modern world of the internet, distributed denial of service attacks, among other kinds of attacks, are available to hire, typically though the dark web. Using these services, someone who wishes to implement a DDoS attack can do so without the need to write and distribute a virus. They simply need to contact one of the various available services and, for a small fee, initiate a distributed denial of service attack against their victim company. The length of the attack is limited only to how much they are willing to pay the organization that controls the group of machines.

These devices combined together are called a botnet. The machines that make up the botnet are typically home computers, consumer routers, cable modems, and even Internet of Things (IoT) devices. The computers are infected by a virus that installs software that manages the needs of the organization that controls the botnet. The cable modems and consumer routers are attacked directly by the botnet operator. These consumer devices typically have minimal patching done to them, if any, and are usually easily attacked and infected. Often the passwords for these devices are well known, making them easy to compromise. These devices can often only be patched by the internet service provider and/or cable company that manages the device, and those ISPs will typically not install patches on the devices as doing so introduces risk, which the providers do not want to take.

Internet of Things devices such as lightbulbs, light switches, thermostats, televisions, refrigerators, ovens, microwaves, washing machines, etc. can all be turned into members of a botnet. These internet-connected devices can be infected in a few ways.

The most complex but highly successful way to infect Internet of Things devices is to compromise the supply chain for the vendor that makes the devices. This is done by either attacking the company with a targeted virus or using an easier approach such as bribing a low-paid worker on the production side to infect an internal machine at the manufacturing facility with a targeted virus that can then install a virus on the master machine that controls the software installed on the devices. This allows the attacker to install their software on the Internet of Things devices sold by the vendor, affecting a large number of devices with little risk to the attacker. The other approach taken is to compromise consumers' cable modems and consumer routers, and from there compromise and infect the Internet of Things devices with a virus.

A question that is frequently raised is, why don't internet service providers simply block this network traffic between the virus and the command-and-control server, or between the virus and the networks that are being attacked?

The answer to this is shockingly straightforward. The network traffic between the virus and the command-and-control servers looks like normal internet web traffic. The network traffic to the command-and-control server is simply web server traffic, either HTTP or HTTPS traffic, which makes the traffic basically impossible to tell apart from normal web traffic.

The network traffic between the compromised machines and the target network also looks like legitimate network traffic, making the network traffic next to impossible to detect amidst normal, legitimate network traffic. Additionally, the ISPs would need to spend large amounts of money to buy the network hardware needed to prevent these sorts of attacks. And this would be at effectively no benefit to the ISP. As these are businesses, there is no justification for spending the money to protect other companies that aren't even customers.

What Do Distributed Denial of Service Appliance Services Do?

A distributed denial of service appliance is typically a hardware device that sits at the edge of the computer network. This allows the device to inspect every network packet that comes from the internet to the network.

DDoS protection appliances are used to protect the network from packet-per-second attacks. These appliances are specifically designed to inspect the network traffic and verify that the packets coming into the network are valid. If they are not valid, then the packets are rejected before they reach the network router. This protects the network router from these kinds of attacks.

When deploying an appliance to protect the network against distributed denial of service attacks, the protection device should be placed at the edge of the network between the internet and the firewall that protects the network. This allows all the network traffic coming to the network from the internet to be inspected before it gets to any other device on the network, as shown in Figure 4-1.

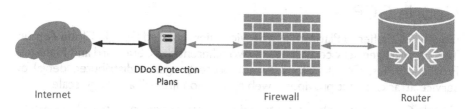

Figure 4-1. Network design with distributed denial of service protection

By placing a distributed denial of service protection device on the network, we can protect network devices against packet-per-second attacks. Byte-per-second attacks won't be mitigated by a protection device. That is because these attacks are based on overloading the network connection between the internet and the network. In order to protect against a byte-per-second attack, the attack needs to be caught at the internet service provider side of the network connection. That is because the goal of these attacks is to fill the network connection between the internet service provider and the company.

The distributed denial of service devices are available as physical devices for on-premises networks. The cloud platform that is being used will determine the distributed denial of service options that are available from the cloud provider.

Microsoft Azure

Microsoft Azure supports a Platform as a Service (PaaS) offering called distributed denial of service protection plans. These protection plans are managed services that can have multiple resources behind them, including vNets, Azure firewalls, application gateways, Azure Bastion, and virtual network gateways, as well as several other resource types. A single distributed denial of service protection plan can be configured to support multiple resources, across multiple subscriptions, across multiple regions.

Amazon AWS

Amazon AWS supports a Platform as a Service offering called AWS Shield. This is a managed service available in two different tiers, Standard and Advanced. AWS Shield Standard is automatically applied to all AWS resources. An additional layer of protection can be added by purchasing AWS Shield Advanced.

AWS Shield Standard includes network and transport layer protections. AWS Shield Advanced adds on additional detection and mitigation against multi-factored distributed denial of service attacks as well as near real-time visibility into any attacks against the infrastructure. AWS Shield Advanced also gives you access to the AWS Shield Response Team as well as protection against spikes in utilization related to distributed denial of service attacks.

Google GCP

Google GCP offers a Platform as a Service offering called Google Cloud Armor. This is a managed service available in two different tiers, Standard and Managed Protection Plus. Google Cloud Armor protects against distributed denial of service attacks, and it provides a web application firewall at a large scale.

Google Cloud Armor also detects and stops attacks against your cloud workloads, preventing web-based workloads using machine learning mechanisms. This protects your virtual machines which are deployed within the GCP platform as well as any other third party products which are deployed within your GCP environment.

What Are the Differences Between Firewalls and Distributed Denial of Service Appliances?

On the surface firewalls and distributed denial of service appliances sound like they do the same thing, but they are actually two very different products, designed to do two very different things. Distributed denial of service protection is often provided via an Intrusion Prevention System (IPS).

Firewalls are designed to stop valid network connections from reaching through to the machines on the other side of the firewall. This can mean stopping network traffic from coming from the internet to the internal machines on the network, or it can mean blocking internet access from machines on the internal network so that those machines cannot access the internet unless the traffic is allowed. This protects the company computers from being accessed from the internet, and it prevents the machines within the company's network from accessing the internet unless those machines are specifically allowed to. By blocking the outbound network traffic to all but specific sites, we can prevent computers that are infected with ransomware or viruses designed to exfiltrate data from being able to access the websites that contain the instructions on what to do once they are installed.

Distributed denial of service prevention appliances, on the other hand, are designed to look for illegitimate network traffic and block that network traffic before it connects to the firewalls. This prevents the firewalls between the internet and the company's network from receiving this network traffic at all.

In a physical environment, these two components will often be two separate devices within the networking rack. Smaller companies may opt for network equipment from vendors that can provide both of these features in a single device. However, it should be noted that it is often better to spend a little bit extra money and have two separate devices to handle these tasks. While having two network devices does increase the cost of the solution, this also increases the company's protection from bad actors on the internet.

When connecting these physical devices, the distributed denial of service device will sit in front of the firewall, which will sit in front of the router, as shown in Figure 4-2.

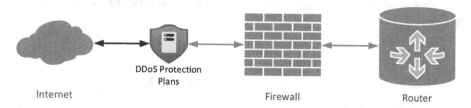

Internet   DDoS Protection   Firewall   Router
                               Plans

Figure 4-2. Network design with distributed denial of service protection and a firewall

If the firewall were to be placed in front of the distributed denial of service appliance, then the firewall would take the full brunt of the network traffic that would normally be stopped by the DDoS appliance. In the event of a packets-per-second DDoS attack against the network, and if the DDoS appliance were behind the firewall, the processor within the firewall could easily become overloaded, preventing other internet users from accessing resources over the internet, and the computers behind the firewall wouldn't be able to access the internet until the attack ended.

Firewalls and Distributed Denial of Service Applications in the Cloud

As you've seen in this chapter and the prior one, all three of the major cloud providers offer both firewall and distributed denial of service offerings for their cloud services.

Microsoft Azure offers their firewall and distributed denial of service offerings as two separate features (Azure Firewall and Azure DDoS), while Amazon AWS and Google GCP both offer both features as a single offering. No matter the cloud platform being used, a firewall offering should be utilized to further isolate the environment from the internet. In some cloud architectures, third-party firewalls from a vendor other than the cloud vendor can be utilized, either alone or in conjunction with the cloud vendor's native firewall product. Using a third-party firewall in conjunction with the native firewall is not typically needed from a technical perspective, but is often a requirement of highly regulated industries.

The network design for a network with this dual firewall setup looks very similar to the design shown in Figure 4-1. The network design shown in Figure 4-3, while specific to Microsoft Azure, would be similar in Amazon's AWS or Google GCP, with slightly different object names, and with the distributed denial of service and native firewall appliances being a single service.

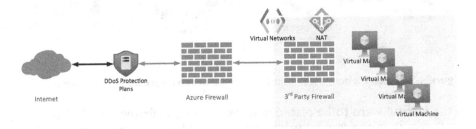

Figure 4-3. Azure network design with a third-party firewall

When using a third-party firewall within Microsoft Azure,[1] the firewall is placed within its own subnet within the virtual network (vNet). A user-defined route (UDR) is then placed on the other subnets that host the virtual machines to route all the network traffic to the third-party firewall. After the network traffic is inspected by the third-party firewall, it is passed to the Azure firewall for secondary network traffic inspection, before the traffic is passed to the internet.

Because the third-party firewall is effectively just a virtual machine, it must sit on a virtual network, and it is managed just like any other virtual machine within the cloud environment. This means that CPU usage, memory usage, and network traffic throughput need to be monitored and sized accordingly for the environment.

Many cloud providers beyond the big three offer the ability to have third-party firewalls and distributed denial of service devices and may require them as opposed to having a first-party Platform as a Service offering.

---

[1] While this example uses Microsoft Azure, this environment could be created with the same basic network design in Amazon's AWS or Google's GCP platforms.

Do I Need a Distributed Denial of Service Appliance?

Whether you need a distributed denial of service appliance is a loaded question. The short answer to this is "probably." If your internet service provider doesn't offer any DDoS protections, then you do. If your internet service provider does offer DDoS protections, then the need for one is a matter of risk acceptance that their service is going to provide you the protection that is needed.

If the provider isn't able to quantify what level of protection they are able to give, then acquiring a distributed denial of service appliance to protect the environment is going to be a wise investment.

Like any security device, the hope is that the device is never going to be needed. But if it is needed, and it isn't available and in place and working, then there is nothing that can be done until the attack is over.

While it seems a little backward, lower-end internet services from the traditional internet service providers will often include some level of distributed denial of service protection, while higher-end dedicated network services from ISPs will not. The more traditional internet service providers service home users, who do not typically have these sorts of devices on their networks. Additionally, the network service providers may be inspecting the network traffic from the home users as the traffic goes to the internet, looking for any denial-of-service traffic from these users, so that the traffic can be blocked. With higher-end services, distributed denial of service offerings will typically not be included but may be available.

In either case, for any site that contains systems that customers need to access, DDoS protection is needed in order to ensure that the network doesn't suffer from a disruption of service in the event of a network issue.

The more publicly accessible and publicly visible the company is, the more appliances or services that do DDoS protection are needed. Large companies all have distributed denial of service protection appliances protecting their inbound network traffic, while the website for Billy Bob's Bate, Tackle, and Roadside diner probably doesn't need this level of protection. Smaller companies, like our good friend Billy Bob, will typically host the online store with a larger company that has this sort of protection as services they offer.

As the geopolitical climate changes,[2] so too must the network protection requirements. Shortly after the invasion of Ukraine by Russia, many companies reported increased attacks on the networks, with those attacks being traced

---

[2] Parts of this book were written just after Russia invaded Ukraine, and the assumptions made in reference to this military action are based on the events up to early March 2022.

back to IP addresses in Russia. Many companies simply blocked network traffic from Russia, either by geo-location or via the published IP addresses assigned to Russia (depending on the capabilities of the firewall vendor). Some companies that had customers or partners blocked access to their services from Russia, with the message to their partners of "Sorry, but you'll need to find another team that isn't based in Russia to handle these requests as your Russia-based team won't be able to connect anymore."

When it comes to protecting the company's assets, proper protection is key. This requires purchasing and deploying the correct solutions. While these solutions aren't the cheapest, their cost is minimal compared to the cost of not having these solutions protecting the company's environment and reputation.

Remote Connectivity

Being able to work remotely from the office is key to a successful workforce. Having a way to securely connect these end users to the company infrastructure is vital, especially in the time of a global pandemic like that which started in early 2020.

Having employees who are working remotely usually means making a giant change in company philosophy. When companies required most or all employees to work in the office, managers and executives often had reasons such as employee productivity and/or staff unity to keep them there. Often, these reasons don't match the employees' experiences at the office, as they can be more productive at home, and many times the "company culture" that managers and executives talk about preserving isn't what they think it is. As we learned during the Covid-19 pandemic, when the vast majority of employees were able to work from home and during the hours that worked the best for them, employees don't need to be in an office to be productive. During this time, lots of companies showed record profits proving just that. Companies such as brick and mortar stores saw a drop in revenue due to the fact that the stores had to be closed for months on end.

© Denny Cherry 2022

D. Cherry, *Enterprise-Grade IT Security for Small and Medium Businesses*, https://doi.org/10.1007/978-1-4842-8628-9_5

This leads to the assumption that managers and executives want to keep their employees in an office as a simple matter of control. Giving the employees the ability to work remotely leads to an increase in employee productivity and an increase in employee satisfaction, which will lead to an increase in company profits, especially when accounting for a reduction in company office space. But giving employees the ability to work remotely means that the work needs to be done in a way that is safe for the company and its information and that will allow for the secure transmission of information between the employees' devices and the company infrastructure.

By ensuring that all information between the employee and the office infrastructure is secure, you ensure that the information the customer has trusted the company with is safe. The company has two basic responsibilities. The first is for the company to make a profit. But in order to do that, the company needs to store and process the information that has been entrusted to it in a safe and secure manner. Storing and maintaining this data safely becomes even more important when a company is trusted with access to information from people who aren't customers, and who many never have even heard of the company.

■ **Note**   That last line is critical in my mind right now. As I was writing this chapter, I received a letter in the mail from some insurance company I had never heard of, which operates on the other side of the United States. This company had suffered a breach where a third-party insurance agent had had their credentials compromised.

This gave the attacker access to several systems the insurance company had, including a third-party system (which I can only assume is a system that provides information from the California Department of Motor Vehicles, as this should be the only system an insurance company should have access to that would have the kind of information they said was potentially viewed.

This leads to this insurance company's now having to pay for credit monitoring services as well as dealing with any potential lawsuits (remember, the affected people are not their customers, so there's no contract requiring binding arbitration or preventing lawsuits) that come up from people who were never customers, and therefore never made the company money.

Needless to say, when the letter arrived I was not impressed, and without trying the company that I've never heard of has lost my faith, and because of that it is a company I'll make a point of never using.

There are a variety of methods that can be used to safely and securely remotely access company systems.

Virtual Private Network

The most common way to access the office network securely is by using a virtual private network (VPN). A virtual private network creates a secure encrypted tunnel between the end user's computer and the company's infrastructure. This connection is encrypted, which prevents anyone from capturing and viewing the network traffic as it travels from the end user's computer to the company's infrastructure. These connections are authenticated, meaning that the users need to provide their username and password in order to connect, as well as have the correct encryption settings to properly secure the connection.

Person-to-Site Virtual Private Network

VPN connections have been an option for decades and provide a safe and secure connection option for companies and users no matter what operating system the user's device is using. This includes the Windows[1] operating system, Apple Computers' Mac OS,[2] and the various flavors of the Linux operating system that are available, as well as connections from cell phones running Google's Android[3] operating system, Apple's iOS,[4] and the other cell phone platforms.

There are a variety of VPN options and services out there. Microsoft Windows supports creating a VPN server using the Routing and Remote Access Services software. Most business network routers also support being a VPN server so that users can connect to the network remotely. No matter which solution is used, the end result is that computers that connect to the virtual private network create a secure, encrypted connection between the user's computer and the VPN server, as shown in Figure 5-1.

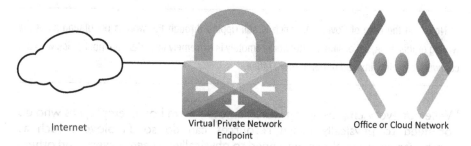

Internet   Virtual Private Network   Office or Cloud Network
                         Endpoint

Figure 5-1. Person-to-site virtual private network

---

[1] Windows is a trademark of the Microsoft Corporation.
[2] Mac OS is a trademark of Apple Computers.
[3] Android is a trademark of the Alphabet Corporation.
[4] iOS is a trademark of Cisco Systems and is used by Apple Computers under license.

Whichever virtual private network solution is used, a variety of encryption options exist, with the highest levels of encryption being unbreakable. However, there is a cost to having such a high level of encryption, which is an increase in processor usage on both the user's computer and the VPN server. Larger organizations will have devices dedicated to being the virtual private network server so that this increased processor utilization doesn't impact other services.

This also allows for companies which are in counties which prohibit the use of higher encryption levels, or which are not able to import higher levels of encryption due to export restrictions of the United States of America.

While the Microsoft Windows Routing and Remote Access Server uses the built-in Windows Virtual Private Network client, the VPNs that are provided by many of the network devices require their own client to be installed and configured. This is because these VPNs support options and features that native Windows virtual private networks do not support, or they require connectivity on different network ports in order to initiate the connection.

Virtual private networks can support network segmentation as if the user were physically located in the office. This gives the same levels of protection whether the user is physically in the company's office, or if they are located on the other side of the planet Earth.

Once the user is connected over the virtual private network they can access whatever resources they need within the organization. This includes the ability to access file shares and internal websites, as well as to connect to Microsoft Windows desktop computers via the Remote Desktop Service, which is a native feature of the Windows operating system. This gives the end users the same access and same feelings as if they were at the office, while working remotely.

■ **Note**   In the time of Covid-19, which is still ripping through the world's population as of the writing of this book, accessing the network remotely is extremely important as most office workers can work remotely instead of being at an office.

While not every employee can work remotely from home, employees who do not need to physically touch resources can do so. Employees such as warehouse workers, those who need to physically manage servers, and others that need to physically touch company resources will need to be in the offices; however, information workers who work online can perform their jobs from anywhere. While they can work from anywhere, it is important for the company to protect itself when having employees working remotely.

Site-to-Site Virtual Private Network

Site-to-site virtual private networks are used to connect different offices and data centers to be connected to each other. Site-to-site VPNs are not used for users to connect to a virtual private network, but instead for two distinct locations to connect to each other securely. Site-to-site VPNs are used to connect remote field offices to the main corporate office, or to connect an office environment to the company's cloud environment, as shown in Figure 5-2.

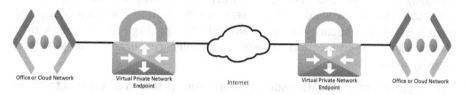

Figure 5-2. Site-to-site virtual private network design

A site-to-site virtual private network is used to connect disparate sites while not having a physical network connecting them. Site-to-site VPNs are used in place of running physical network connections between sites, as unless the buildings are physically close to each other the cost of digging the trenches and running network cables between sites is cost prohibitive, except for the largest of companies.

These site-to-site virtual private networks can be used to allow resources within one company site to connect to resources within another company site. This allows the company to have a wide open network between sites, or to have any network rules that are needed to allow or prevent network traffic between the sites.

Third-Party Desktop Sharing Services

There are a variety of third-party desktop sharing systems available. These third-party systems create an unnecessary security risk as the third-party company gains access to computers within the company's network. If these services are compromised the attacker could gain access to internal resources. There are a variety of safe, secure solutions available for companies to deploy, such as a virtual desktop infrastructure (VDI), like Azure Virtual Desktop (which is discussed later in this chapter) or Application Publishing, using the App-V features of the Windows operating system, which also requires the use of a virtual private network.

Depending on how these third-party services are configured and depending on what part of their infrastructure is compromised, multiple machines within the environment could become compromised.

While it may seem like these services provide a secure way to access internal resources, the risk of using them is too high. Any service or system that isn't under the control of the company and gains access to the company's resources is problematic at the very least.

While these services advertise that they provide a secure way into your company, they open a connection between the desktop computer on which their software is installed and the service's machines. The basic design of these systems is a security issue, as any software package that is designed to maintain an open connection between companies' resources is going to be a security issue.

These systems must maintain such a connection, as they are designed to allow you to connect to the computer from any web browser. This requires that the service maintain a connection to the computer at all times so that the user is able to access their computer at any time. This means that there is a third-party service that is only going to allow the authored user (according to them) to connect.

When it comes to IT security, the risk when using a third-party service to grant this sort of remote desktop access is simply too great. System administrators can ensure that access to these systems is prevented by blocking access to them from company computers. This is done by putting rules in the company's firewalls that prevent access to these systems so that in the event that users attempt to go to these services' websites they are not able to do so.

The best way to prevent these sorts of solutions from being used is to provide a solution that fits the needs of the employees. This could be a virtual private network, such as was described earlier in this chapter, or a remote desktop service, such as the Azure Virtual Desktop service, which is described next.

Azure Virtual Desktop

Microsoft Azure has a service available called Azure Virtual Desktop. This service allows you to create virtual computers within the Microsoft Azure cloud environment. These virtual machines can be configured with a Windows desktop operating system, such as Windows 10 or Windows 11, and can have any software needed installed on them. The Microsoft Azure environment can be configured to have a site-to-site virtual private network linking to the office network. This allows any information transmitted over the connection to the office to be encrypted, which prevents anyone from monitoring the connection.

The Azure Virtual Desktop service can be configured to provide the employee either a normal Windows desktop, so the user can install software and use the virtual machine, or the virtual machine can have specific software installed on it, and that software can be published so that the user has an icon for the specific software when they log in to the service.

Users can access the Azure Virtual Desktop environment using a desktop software package that can be installed on their computer or accessed via a web-based solution. In either case, the connection is secure, and there is no persistent connection between the user's office computer and a third-party service. The software that is accessed via the service is stored securely in the cloud, and is only accessible when the user connects to the service.

Authentication to the service is provided by Microsoft's Azure Active Directory. Active Directory can be configured with multi-factor authentication using the Microsoft Authentication service (or other third-party multi-factor authentication) software package (multi-factor authentication is discussed later in this book).

The Microsoft Azure Virtual Desktop service can be configured with as few or as many virtual machines as needed. The virtual machines can be configured using just about any machine size available within the Azure platform. When configuring the virtual machines and the Azure Virtual Desktop environment, multiple users can be configured per virtual machine, and the Azure Virtual Desktop platform will ensure that the configured number of users, at maximum, will be connected to each virtual machine.

The Azure Virtual Desktop environment can be configured in a variety of Azure regions, with users configured to connect to the Azure Virtual Desktop environment within the region physically closest to them. This allows users to use the published applications with the least possible network latency between the end user and the Azure Virtual Desktop platform. By reducing network latency as much as possible, the users of the Azure Virtual Desktop platform will receive the best-performing platform possible with as few network performance issues as possible.

The Azure Virtual Desktop platform can be configured with auto-scale features, which allow the platform to scale up as needed as users connect to it. This automatic scaling of the platform allows for a well-performing virtual desktop environment while keeping the cost of the platform at the lowest possible cost per month.

Azure Virtual Desktop contains several individual components. At the core of these components are virtual machines, which are all connected to an Azure virtual network. This Azure virtual network would then typically have a site-to-site virtual private network configured to allow the Azure Virtual Desktop environment to connect to the office or colocation network, as shown in Figure 5-3.

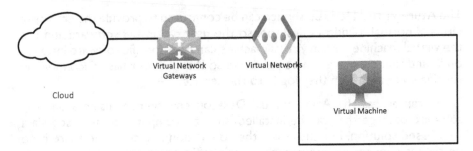

Figure 5-3. Azure Virtual Desktop basic network diagram

When creating the Azure Virtual Desktop environment, several different components are created. These components increase backend pools, which are made up of the Azure virtual machines. Workspaces are created within the Azure Virtual Desktop and define how backend pools are mapped together. The Azure Virtual Desktop environment also includes application pools, which define the application that the user is going to connect to by pointing to a specific application or to the desktop of the virtual machines.

The Computers

Computer Operating System Security

There are three major computer operating system families that run every desktop and server computer in the world. These are the Windows operating system made by Microsoft, the Mac OS operating system made by Apple Computer, and the *nix (pronounced "nuxs") operating system, which breaks down into two categories: Linux and Unix. Linux and Unix are distributed by a variety of companies, each slightly different from the others. These versions of the operating system are called distributions. While these distributions are all slightly different, they are all based off the same foundation. Over the years Apple has made a couple of different operating systems depending on which hardware the computer is running. Older versions are referred to as the Apple Operating System while the newer versions are called Mac OS. Some people use the names interchangeably.

The base of the *nix operating system is a piece of code called the Kernel. The Kernel provides the interface from the software to the hardware, such as the USB ports, PCI cards, and other hardware components, as well as manages the processes, memory, hard drive storage input/output requests, and so forth. Linux Kernels are generally based off of an open source Kernel that is

© Denny Cherry 2022
D. Cherry, *Enterprise-Grade IT Security for Small and Medium Businesses*,
https://doi.org/10.1007/978-1-4842-8628-9_6

available for free to companies to modify and distribute, with certain limitations based on the license that is used.

The Microsoft Windows and Apple operating systems each also have a Kernel. The Microsoft Windows Kernel was developed by the Microsoft Corporation, while the Apple operating system's Kernel was developed by two different companies, depending on which version of the Apple OS is being used. Older versions use a Kernel developed by Apple Computers, while newer versions are based on a Kernel written by Berkey Software Distribution (BSD).

In the end, all of these operating systems, no matter what company developed them, provide the basic requirement. They provide an interface between the software running on the computer and the hardware that is installed.

Apple Computer makes not only the software that runs on their computers, but also the hardware platforms. This gives them great control over the entire ecosystem as they don't need to support third-party hardware or, most important, third-party software drivers.

Microsoft makes a small portion of the hardware used by their software. This hardware is available through the Windows Surface hardware line. This gives Microsoft greater control of the ecosystem for these devices, but they also support a wide variety of computer hardware available on the market. Microsoft works closely with the major computer companies, such as HP, Dell, IBM, Lenovo, etc., to ensure that their software works with well with the hardware companies' hardware.

The various companies that have *nix distributions do not produce their own hardware. They simply support a variety of hardware that is available on the market. Some of these companies have agreements to work with hardware companies such as HP, Dell, IBM, and Lenovo, as well as others.

Microsoft Windows makes up the vast majority of desktop operating systems, followed by Apple and *nix operating systems. On the server side of the information technology market, the *nix operating systems dominate the market, with Microsoft Windows taking a large minority share. Apple Computer does not have any recordable portion of the information technology server market as they do not have a server version of their operating system nor of their computer hardware.

Security Updates

No matter the operating system, and no matter which company developed it, updates are required for a variety of reasons, including software security updates, software enhancements, or fixes for software bugs discovered after the software was released.

Security bugs are something that happens in the software world. The more complex the software, the greater the risk of bugs' being introduced in the software. Computer software is written by people, and people are fallible. Computer operating systems are made up of millions if not billions of lines of computer code, and small errors can be introduced in that code that need to be patched through regular updates.

Updates for all computer security platforms are made available through the software companies' regular update channels. These fixes are then rolled into the future versions of the operating system, which also include other enhancements and improvements.

*nix Security

Updates to the *nix operating systems are the most hard to define as each company that has released a distribution has its own update process to release software updates for its operating system. In the modern computer world these updates are released via the internet. Depending on the software distribution, you may be able to download the updates directly from the vendor, or you may need to stand up your own patching infrastructure to download the patches and distribute them to the various computers.

Companies generally select a single *nix distribution in order to simplify the management and patching of their systems. Not all companies select a single vendor. Many of the *nix distributions are free, while some are available for a fee. These pay versions include support. Some companies will use a free, non-supported distribution of *nix for the majority of systems while using a paid for, supported distribution of for critical systems such as database servers and other systems that are key to the organization's operations.

No matter the distribution or the process involved, patching of the servers is critical in order to solve security issues that arise.

Many of the distributions have patching infrastructures that can be installed on computers to allow the software patches to be cached and the installation of the software to be controlled and scheduled by group of servers. The actual functioning of this software will vary depending on how it was designed. The base process of the software will all be the same; computers are grouped so that the patch installation to the computers is controlled and monitored.

Windows Security

Microsoft provides security patches for their Windows operating system through the Windows Update platform. Computers can download the updates directly from Microsoft using Windows Update, or companies can build their own patching environment to download the updates and deploy them to the computers.

Microsoft has released a couple of different patching platforms called Endpoint Production Manager and Windows Server Update Services (WSUS). Endpoint Production Manager used to be called System Center Configuration Manager (SCCM); however, it was rebranded in 2021.

The most important difference between Endpoint Protection Manager and WSUS is that Endpoint Protection Manager is a paid service, while WSUS is included with the Windows operating system. Because of the cost associated with Endpoint Protection Manager, typically only large companies use the platform.

The Windows Server Update Services, unlike what the name sounds like, does not patch only the Windows Server operating system; it also patches the desktop operating system that is installed on desktops and laptops.

The WSUS platform allows you to group computers together and deploy updates to those computers by group. One of the important factors that WSUS allows for is approval of updates before those updates are deployed to the computers. This allows an administrator to approve the updates before they are installed.

Many companies will group computers together for Windows Server Update Services as follows:

- Desktops - IT
- Desktops - All
- Servers – Development
- Servers – Quality Assurance
- Servers – Production
- Servers – Disaster Recovery

By placing their computers in these groups, or groups similar to these, the company is able to control how software patches are distributed to the computers, ensuring that the Windows computers are patched while doing so at the lowest risk to the company.

The desktop computers (both desktops and laptops) are broken into two groups, one with the IT team's desktops and one with the rest of the company's desktops. This allows the patches to be installed to the IT team's desktops first to ensure that the patches work without interrupting the business. The idea behind this process is to ensure if there is any issue it will affect only the information technology team and not the company at large. This means that in the event that there is a problem where the Windows patch conflicts with the company's software, or there is a major bug in a patch, it will only impact the IT team and not the rest of the company. The rest of the company can continue working while a new patch is released and tested. Information technology people like to be the first to have their machines patched for two reasons:

1. The IT team members can more easily troubleshoot any problems that come from the patches.

2. The IT team members can often work around the issues that arise from potential problems with the various patches.

The servers are broken into several different groups again to ensure that the production servers used to run the company are patched with only known good patches. This allows the patches to be installed on the development servers and then tested before they are installed on the quality assurance (QA) servers, which are then tested. Once everything is verified to be tested and working on the development and quality assurance servers, the patches can be approved and installed on the production servers, then finally on the disaster recovery servers. This separation of software installation allows the greatest chance of the patches' being successfully installed on the production servers without having any impact on the operations of the company.

Sadly, this level of testing of patches is required. Software patches, like any other computer software, can have bugs as well as unintended consequences, such as when those patches are used on computers that have other software installed on them.

There is a variety of third-party patching software options available that perform the same function as the Windows Server Update Services. These third-party software packages have more-streamlined interfaces and processes. WSUS, to be used to its full potential, requires several servers and caching updates on multiple servers, one server per patching group. With the third-party packages, this can all be performed typically within a single server.

Apple Security

Apple Computers, much like the other companies that make operating systems, requires patching to ensure that its computers are up to date and as safe as possible. These patches are distributed over the Internet and are available for download by the users of the Mac OS.

Because Apple does not make server software, they do not have a patching infrastructure like Microsoft Windows or the *nix distributions.

Is Windows or Linux Better?

Which operating system is best is an age-old discussion similar to which beer is better, Budweiser or Coors; or which American car is better, Ford or Chevy; or which Dutch beer is better, Amstel or Heineken?

Some people have an absolute love for one platform over the other, sometimes to a religious extreme.

The *nix[1] lovers will point out that Windows has had more bugs and breaches than *nix has had. But when we look at the number, it makes more sense that Windows has had more bugs discovered. Because Windows is the dominant platform for desktop computers, the Windows operating system is installed on a huge number of computers compared to *nix platforms. This gives attackers a huge financial advantage when it comes to attacking the Windows operating system versus another platform.

Microsoft Windows is also a victim of its own success. Because Microsoft Windows has become so successful with the general public, and it has become so easy to operate and manage that anyone can do it, not everyone operates it the most securely. The *nix platform, on the other hand, isn't as easy to manage or configure. The *nix platform requires editing of configuration files via a text editor while the Microsoft Windows platform provides a graphical user interface (GUI) for most functions. Because of this, there are a large number of people that mange Windows servers who are not experts in IT security, while a large number of the people who manage *nix servers are very well versed in IT security.

Due to this disparity in the average skills of the people managing these systems, the Microsoft operating system has earned itself a bad reputation. With each newer version of Windows, security issues and software bugs are resolved. This can be seen most readily in the differences between Windows 95 / Windows 98 and the Windows 2000 platform. In the hands of someone who knows how to properly configure Windows servers, Windows can be made just as secure as *nix. Similarly, someone who doesn't know how to properly use the *nix operating system can easily configure the OS to be extremely insecure.

So, the question here isn't which platform is the best, as they are effectively the same. The difference comes down to who will be managing the system. Those who don't have a lot of experience with a platform are bound to make misconfigurations, and those misconfigurations can lead to serious vulnerabilities. Those people are where the biggest differences between the platforms are shown.

---

[1] For the purposes of this section, the Apple operating system falls into the *nix bucket, as the current version of the Apple OS is based on the BSD flavor of Linux.

Minimizing the Attack Surface

One key to information technology security is the concept of minimizing the attack surface. This means that to protect the company's IT assets the systems need to be configured with the minimum number of services connected to the internet. Computers use a software configuration called network ports to establish communication. These network ports are how computers talk to each other. There are commonly used network ports, which are used by people to connect to known services such as web pages, which listen on TCP Port 80, and secure web pages, which listen on TCP Port 443.

Note There are three primary network protocols used by computers: TCP, UDP, and ICMP. TCP is used for most communications to network services, such as web servers, database servers, etc., as the TCP protocol involves two-way communications with responses to traffic.

UDP network traffic is a more one-way communication style, more like when speaking to a group over a bullhorn and no response is expected.

The ICMP network protocol is used to verify that a network device is responding, and to trace the path the network connection makes between the client device and the server.

While web pages can be configured to use other network ports, this would mean that users wouldn't be able to connect to the web server without knowing the network port. As an example, if www.cnn.com were to change their network port from 80 to 81, people wouldn't be able to access the CNN webpage at http://www.cnn.com. Instead, they would need to tell their web browser is connect to TCP Port 81 instead using the URL http://www.cnn.com:81/. This makes the website much harder for the users to connect to and access, while doing very little to stop the attackers from accessing the site. This is because as soon as the general public knows that the website has been moved to another port, the attackers will learn of this change as well.

The attack surface of the servers can be minimized by using firewalls and DDoS devices, as discussed in earlier chapters in this book. The firewalls allow network traffic to network ports to be blocked unless it should be specifically allowed.

In addition to blocking network traffic, administrators can remove software from the server that isn't needed to complete the needed task. This means that web servers should only be web servers, and database servers should only be database servers. While this causes the company's footprint to increase, meaning that there will be more servers installed, this is a small price to pay for a more secure environment.

Using servers for multiple purposes often happens in Windows server environments as it is very easy to configure Windows servers to handle multiple tasks. However, this can introduce security issues, and increase the number of patches that need to be installed on the individual servers. As an example, web servers shouldn't have database servers installed on them. They also shouldn't have Microsoft Office installed. Having these packages installed on the web server doesn't do anything to improve the performance of the website that is hosted on the server, and requires that these packages have software updates installed on them.

Data Encryption

Data encryption is the process of scrambling the data so that it can't be intercepted or read by someone other than the intended recipient. At its most basic level, data encryption is a mathematical process by which data is processed in order to come out with a scrambled version of the data. One of the key requirements of data encryption is that the encrypted information must be able to be decrypted so that the normal text data can be displayed to the user.

Data encryption is used in our everyday lives. Whenever we purchase anything online, the website is encrypted using either Secure Socket Layer (SSL) or Transport Layer Security (TLS). When encrypting data, a key needs to be provided that is used as part of the encryption process. Web servers that provide encrypted websites have security certificates installed on them. These certificates provide that key to ensure that the data is secured in transit. The certificate provides two different keys: one is a public key, and one is a private key. The private key is what is used to encrypt the data, and the public key is given to the client computer (in this case the user's web browser) so that the data can be decrypted.

The user is able to trust that the web page they are viewing is the actual website they think they are visiting, because the certificate that is used to sign the encryption process is authorized to only be used on that website. If a different certificate were used, the website would present an error message that the certificate was for a different website than the one that the user was visiting.

In modern days, getting a certificate for a company's website is extremely inexpensive, if not free. It is expected today that all websites will be secured by certificates and encryption. It is so expected that global search engines such as Google reduce a website's ranking if the website doesn't have a certificate installed.

Data encryption isn't limited to just websites. Data within databases and files on file servers can be encrypted as well. With data encryption within a database, the data is protected so people who don't have the encryption key can't view the data. The keys to decrypt the data are typically stored on the application server or the web server so that the data is both stored in the database in the encrypted form and then transferred to the web server, when it is decrypted, so that it can be prepared to be viewed by the user (the data is encrypted again before it is transmitted to the user, assuming that the web server is set up to use a certificate). This level of encryption ensures that anyone who downloads the database, or connects to the database server and requests to view data from the database, is presented with only encrypted data and not a readable version of the data.

Encryption can also be deployed to file servers to protect files stored on the file server. The files are stored by using an encryption process, and when the files need to be viewed by an authorized user, the files are decrypted and transferred to the user's application (such as Microsoft Word or Microsoft Excel). This protects the files that are stored on the file server by the files' failing to open without the key. If the attacker downloads the files to their computer, the attacker wouldn't have the key, and therefore wouldn't be able to open the downloaded files.

Encryption of data is basically the gold standard when it comes to safely storing data within the IT world, so long as the encryption that is being used is safe and secure.

Not all encryption algorithms are created equal. Over time, older encryption options are considered insecure. This change in their status, from able to unable to secure data, comes from one of two factors:

1. Errors in algorithms that weren't exploitable with older, slower hardware are now exploitable.

2. Key length of the older algorithms makes brute-force attacks possible.

These two factors have one thing in common: as computer hardware has gotten faster over time, the older algorithms have become easier to bypass. The increase in computing system power over time can be expressed through Moore's Law, which states the following:

The number of transistors on a microchip double roughly every two years, though the cost is halved.

—*Gordon Moore, 1965*

As computer processing power has increased over the years, the amount of time needed to brute force the encryption key has decreased, by roughly half of the time every two years.

When you use brute force to figure out the password or encryption key, you are effectively trying every possible key, usually in alphabetical order, until you find the password or encryption key that matches and lets you decrypt the data. These brute-force attacks are scripted so that they run as quickly as possible. In some cases the attacker will use a distributed system to decrease the amount of time needed to brute force the password. This leads to another reason why the older algorithms are no longer considered secure.

The amount of processing power available to an attacker today compared to 5 to 10 years ago is massively different. Ten years ago an attacker would have run the brute-force attack on their own machine, or if they had access to a botnet of computers via a virus that infected computers, they could use that botnet. In the modern times of the cloud, an attacker could use a stolen credit card number to create a cloud account in any one of the big three cloud platforms, or on one of the smaller third-party cloud platforms. Once the cloud account was created the attacker would have access to effectively limitless numbers of VMs and CPUs (especially in the larger cloud platforms), which they could then use to brute force the password or encryption key.

The newer versions of the encryption algorithms use longer, often much longer, keys, which increases the amount of time needed to brute force these passwords and/or encryption keys.

When setting up passwords for encryption, or really any password in general, the password should be as long as possible. Short passwords are certainly easier to remember, but remembering the passwords isn't the goal; the goal is to create a secure password where the password can't be brute forced in any reasonable amount of time. As brute-force processes typically go in alphabetical order of passwords and/or encryption keys, the longer the password the longer it will take to brute force it, and therefore the greater the chance that the attacker will become bored of waiting and move on to an easier target.

One of the realities of data encryption, because the encryption can eventually be broken, is that the goal is really to make breaking the encryption take enough time that the attacker simply gets bored and moves on to an easier target. While this isn't the technical goal of using encryption on sensitive data, it is a reality.

Many jurisdictions have data protection laws, which often include some sort of requirement that data be encrypted. To date, these laws don't specify what sort of encryption, or what strength encryption is to be used, but there are some major benefits to having your data be encrypted.

Several of the data protection laws passed in recent years in the United States require that if there is a data breach (usually defined as the data's being accessed by a person not authorized by the company) and the data is not encrypted then all of the customers need to be notified of the data breach, and there are potential fines that the company needs to then pay. There may even be a requirement that the company disclose the breach publicly. If, however, the data is encrypted, under some of the state laws the company doesn't need to notify their customers, or even disclose to the public that the data breach happened.

■ **Note**   When I was working at an auto-finance company several years ago, we had an Oracle database administrator whose spouse was also an Oracle database administrator. The company's database administrator resigned and became a contractor for the company. As a contractor they were able to work from home. It turned out that the contractor gave their credentials to their spouse, and their spouse was the one actually connecting to our systems and using our company email to respond to people.

The first thought when reading this story is that this person should have been working from the office, not from home. However, there are plenty of ways that a person could have someone else (a spouse in this case) connect remotely even while in the office, and have the spouse do their work, while the person in question works on other company's systems via VPN.

As soon as the company discovered what was happening, the contractor's accounts were disabled. I remember walking into my manager's office and informing him that this might qualify as a data breach under California state law, and he literally put his head on his desk, sat there for a minute, and then called the legal team to bring them up to speed.

The legal team, after reviewing the applicable state laws (the company did business in 49 states) and the fact that the data within the database was all encrypted, and the consultant didn't have access to the encryption keys, determined that the company didn't meet the requirements for notification of the public or our customers because of this. The key reason that we didn't have to notify customers, according to the legal team, was because the data stored within the database was encrypted.

Multi-Factor Authentication

Any company that isn't using multi-factor authentication (MFA), and using it correctly, is basically failing at information technology security right off the bat.

The concept of multi-factor authentication is fairly old these days, but still is often used incorrectly or not at all. The idea behind MFA is that to log in you need to know something, your username and password, and you have to have something—typically your cell phone or a multi-factor authentication fob, such as a YurbiKey or a smart card.

A properly set up MFA system using a cell phone will have an application installed on the phone. There are a wide variety of these applications available from a variety of companies, such as the following:

- Microsoft Authenticator
- Duo Mobile
- FortiToken Mobile
- SalesForce Authenticator
- Google Authenticator

© Denny Cherry 2022
D. Cherry, *Enterprise-Grade IT Security for Small and Medium Businesses*,
https://doi.org/10.1007/978-1-4842-8628-9_7

These applications all work basically the same way. Some applications require a specific multi-factor authentication application, while others can use just about any MFA application. Azure Active Directory, for example, requires the use of the Microsoft Authenticator application in order to use all of the features of the MFA sign-in process, but other applications can be used. The Duo multi-factor authentication process requires the use of the Duo Mobile application on the phone, as does the Fortinet multi-factor authentication process when using their routers for VPN.

Note   I have four different multi-factor authentication applications installed on my phone. But this is because I'm an IT consultant. Most people will have a single MFA app installed on their phone. Within Microsoft Authenticator, MFA is done for 15+ different accounts for various clients. The point here is that a single application can be used to secure more than one account.

Often when setting up multi-factor authentication, companies (often public websites) will configure your email address for the MFA process instead of having you use a proper multi-factor authentication application. The sending of emails with multi-factor authentication codes is not any more secure than not having MFA enabled at all, *unless* the email account itself is secured by multi-factor authentication.

Using MFA, if it is set up correctly, is extremely easy. You log in to the website or application like normal with your username and password. Once you are successfully logged in, you'll be presented with a screen that prompts you for some sort of multi-factor authentication, as shown in Figure 7-1.

Figure 7-1. Sample multi-factor authentication prompt

In this case, the website is a Microsoft website, specifically the Office 365 portal (https://www.office.com), and it has sent a push notification to my phone similar to that shown in Figure 7-2.

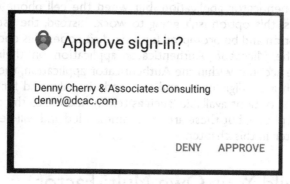

Figure 7-2. Multi-factor authentication prompt on a cell phone

If I am expecting the multi-factor authentication prompt, than I press Approve, and either enter my phone's password or use my fingerprint to authenticate to the phone that I am actually me. If I start to get unexpected multi-factor authentication prompts to my cell phone, then I know that my password has been compromised and that I need to go and change my account.

■ **Note**   Thankfully, I have never gotten unexpected multi-factor authentication prompts.

Push notifications to the multi-factor authentication application aren't the only option for a proper MFA sign-in. In fact, push notifications may not be an option at all in some situations. Cell-phone signal may be poor or not available; for example, on an airplane flight when the user's laptop is connected to the airplane's Wi-Fi, but their cell phone isn't. In cases like these, another login method is needed that doesn't require the cell phone to have internet access. This is where the "I can't use my Microsoft Authentication app right now" link shown in Figure 7-1 comes in. When the user clicks this link, they are offered other ways to get the MFA code, as shown in Figure 7-3.

Figure 7-3. Options to receive a multi-factor authentication code from the Microsoft Authenticator application

The first option listed in Figure 7-3 is to receive a push notification to the Microsoft Authenticator application, but when the cell phone doesn't have internet access, this option isn't going to work. Instead, the user can select the second option and be prompted for a six-digit code. This code is available from inside the Microsoft Authenticator application on their phone. By clicking on the account within the Authenticator application, the user will be presented with a six-digit code, and that code is only valid for 60 seconds. There are other options available, such as texting a code to the cell phone or calling the cell phone, but these aren't recommended and will be discussed in more detail later in this chapter.

Don't Build Your Own Multi-Factor Authentication System

One trap that companies fall into is thinking that they need to build out their own multi-factor authentication system. They do this because they want to control the entire authentication process, which is a feeling that I understand. However, there are a lot of really good, open, third-party authentication platforms hosted by reputable companies that can be used for authentication of your application and that fulfill the multi-factor authentication requirements.

Building your own MFA process will more than likely not be as secure as a third-party multi-factor authentication process, and it is easy to build gaps into the process, or even not actually build a multi-factor authentication process at all.

One client of ours was given some bad information by a third party on the cost of Microsoft Azure Active Directory authentication for their application. Because of this, they decided to build their own multi-factor authentication system using their third-party offshore development team. After two years of development the login process that was presented didn't support multi-factor authentication at all. You had the option of logging in with your password **or** having the system text you a six-digit code to log in. The key word there being the word *or*, which takes their multi-factor authentication system they had built back to a single-factor authentication system, making the system no more secure than it had been two years prior. The only difference is that they got to pay for two years of development time to build the system.

Login and authentication systems like Microsoft's Azure Active Directory platform are very open and usable by just about any application. All that's needed is just a few lines of code within the application to redirect the authentication process to Azure Active Directory. There are connections to Azure Active Directory written for a variety of published applications, including applications like WordPress, the popular blogging and website management platform, which can use Azure Active Directory and multi-factor authentication.

Another part of the login process that often gets forgotten when building your own authentication process is login failure detection and blocking after several failed login attempts in a row. In the event that a user's account is being attacked by a brute-force attack, the system needs to identify that the user has had multiple failed logins, and their account should be disabled automatically for a period of time in order to prevent additional failed logins (which are all attempts to get the user's password), potentially with an email to the user notifying them of the failures.

Failures to log in are part of running a public system. The longer the system has been available, and the longer the user's email address (or username) has been active, the more likely it is that it will be the target of malicious login attempts. As you can see in Figure 7-4, either I'm really bad at logging into my own Office 365 account, and I'm a world traveler, or various people (most probably scripts) are attempting to log in to my account.

Date	↑↓	User	↑↓	Application	↑↓	Status	Location
3/25/2022, 6:01:47 AM		Denny Cher...		Office 365 Exchange Online		Failure	Mariinskiy Posad, Chuvashiya, RU
3/25/2022, 5:47:49 AM		Denny Cher...		Office 365 Exchange Online		Failure	Buffalo, New York, US
3/24/2022, 7:25:51 PM		Denny Cher...		Office 365 Exchange Online		Failure	Surok, Mariy-El, RU
3/23/2022, 3:20:39 AM		Denny Cher...		Office 365 Exchange Online		Failure	Buffalo, New York, US
3/21/2022, 10:19:53 AM		Denny Cher...		Office 365 Exchange Online		Failure	Santa Clara, California, US
3/21/2022, 8:57:57 AM		Denny Cher...		Office 365 Exchange Online		Failure	Buffalo, New York, US
3/21/2022, 5:44:33 AM		Denny Cher...		Office 365 Exchange Online		Failure	Buffalo, New York, US
3/20/2022, 1:32:53 AM		Denny Cher...		Office 365 Exchange Online		Failure	Buffalo, New York, US
3/19/2022, 11:23:36 PM		Denny Cher...		Office 365 Exchange Online		Failure	Buffalo, New York, US
3/19/2022, 7:28:32 PM		Denny Cher...		Office 365 Exchange Online		Failure	Los Angeles, California, US
3/18/2022, 11:37:07 AM		Denny Cher...		Office 365 Exchange Online		Failure	Amsterdam, Noord-Holland, NL

Figure 7-4. Office 365 sign-in logs

When Should MFA Be Used?

The answer to when multi-factor authentication should be used comes down to a very short answer: always. Any time you want to make it much, much harder, if not impossible, to breach an account, multi-factor authentication is going to be the way to do it. When properly implemented, the combination of something you know (your password) and something you have (the authentication application on your cell phone) is next to impossible to beat.

This all requires that the multi-factor authentication be set up correctly and that it doesn't rely on any services that aren't protected by MFA.

Several years ago, we had a client for whom we had done work on occasion. They decided to set up multi-factor authentication without getting advice or information from our team. The CEO of the company set up MFA to text message the CEO's cell phone the MFA codes, which would then be entered into the website on login. The other big problem with their setup was that they had set up their personal email as a recovery email that could be used to reset their company account, and their personal email wasn't set up with multi-factor authentication.

■ **Caution** Every account that's used as part of a multi-factor authentication process needs to be protected by multi-factor authentication.

As their personal account wasn't protected by multi-factor authentication, this allowed attackers a way into their account. The attacker in this case was able to force a password reset using the compromised personal email address. The next problem for the attacker was the MFA. When the attacker logged in to the user's account, they would have been presented with a screen similar to that shown in Figure 7-5.

Figure 7-5. Multi-factor authentication via SMS

The screenshot shown in Figure 7-5 clearly shows that a text message was sent to the user's cell phone. To get past this, the attacker needs the user's cell phone—or do they? In this case, the attacker was able to call the cell phone provider (I imagine that they called the three big providers in the United States until they found the correct one) and convince the customer service representative that they were the CEO of our client. The attacker had the cell phone company move the phone number to a different SIM card, effectively turning the attacker's cell phone into the CEO's cell phone. They then logged in to the Office 365 account with the username and password of the CEO, and they were sent the text message with the six-digit code, which they entered into the website, getting them access to the CEO's account.

Once they were authenticated, they were able to start downloading the CEO's contact list and start sending out emails as the CEO to everyone in the list.

In this case, the CEO was clearly singled out and attacked. The attackers were in the United States, as they were able to get the cell phone provider to switch the phone number to a different SIM card, which would have at least required a U.S. SIM card, and the probability is that they were in the United States.

This could have been avoided if the multi-factor authentication was set up to use the Microsoft Authenticator application and not text messages. The reason for this is that push notifications are not reliant on your cell phone number; they are reliant on the actual cell phone. If you switch to a new cell phone, the multi-factor authentication push notifications will still be sent to the old cell phone. If the old cell phone is connected to Wi-Fi, it will still get the messages. In order to have the push notifications sent to the new cell phone, the application would need to be reregistered with the Microsoft Azure Active Directory system, which would require the Microsoft Authenticator application on the old phone.

The second problem with the CEO's configuration was that a non-multi-factor mailbox was used for password recovery of their work email. If this mailbox had been configured for multi-factor authentication, then the attacker wouldn't have been able to reset the password of the CEO's work email account. But because of a couple of simple misconfiguration errors, MFA appeared to have failed, when in fact it worked exactly as it should have; the attacker just found weaknesses in the configuration that was being employed, and was able to exploit those weaknesses.

Text Messages versus Multi-Factor Authentication Applications

Many multi-factor authentication solutions are built around getting text messages, with the codes that are used after a successful login being sent via text message. However, as we saw earlier in this chapter, relying on text messaging has its flaws. It is depressingly easy to intercept the text messages that are going to a cell phone. On top of that, text messages don't fit the definition of "something you have" that multi-factor authentication relies on, as the text message may be sent to something other than "something you have." Because push notifications are sent to a specific device and not to whatever device happens to have the phone number, the push notifications provide a far superior security configuration and frankly a better user experience, as approving the login requires only clicking the Approve button (see Figure 7-2) as opposed to entering a six-digit code that was texted to you.

All too many companies rely on multi-factor authentication codes' being texted or emailed to you. Every bank I work with in the United States sends text messages for verification.

■ **Caution**   The banks all provide a calling option, which reads you the six-digit code, but this calling method has the same weaknesses as the text messaging solution.

The same goes for the pharmacies that I've used, United States–based retirement programs, hotel chains, etc. As a whole, the information technology industry needs to do better by recommending solutions and having their companies implement solutions that don't just look secure, but actually are secure. These are the solutions that the end users use, but they have security gaps that can lead to accounts' being compromised.

Bypassing Multi-Factor Authentication

There are ways to bypass multi-factor authentication. However, they do require that the user's password be compromised. Multi-factor authentication is supposed to be providing protection at this point.

Brute Forcing Past Multi-Factor Authentication

One of the problems with multi-factor authentication is that, if a user's password is compromised, it can cause the user's phone to become a major nuisance. In the event that the user's password is compromised and an attacker is able to get into the account far enough to be stopped by multi-factor authentication, a push notification, if configured, will be sent to the user's cell phone. The attacker can then log in to the account repeatedly until the user approves the request to simply make the constant notifications stop. Attackers will time the attacks so that the notifications happen late at night or early in the morning. The idea behind this is that the user will be woken up by the noise of the notifications, but not enough for them to realize what they are clicking on, and the user in their groggy state approves the notifications. Once the user has approved the authentication, the attacker can disable MFA or set it up to use their own device instead of the user's device.

Giving the Help Desk Person Who Calls a Multi-Factor Authentication Code

When text messages are sent to the user via text message, it seems like the text message contents should be safe. However, this isn't the case. In the event that the user's account is compromised, the attacker can get that code. The easiest way for the attacker to get that code is to have the user give the code to the attacker over the phone.

This is most easily done by the attacker's calling the user and explaining how they work for the company's help desk and that they need to fix something, but it order to do so they'll need the user to confirm that they are the employee. To verify their account, the attacker will trigger the system to send a code to them. The attacker will then log in to the user's account, which then sends the user a multi-factor authentication code, which the user will then read to the attacker.

The attacker then thanks the user, and then pretends to push some updates to the user's computer. But the attacker has what they need: they have access to the user's account.

Protecting Multi-Factor Authentication

These attacks, and other methods of bypassing multi-factor authentication, can be prevented not by technical methods, but by user education. When MFA push notifications or text messages come and aren't expected, the user should change their password right away and ignore the notifications. If the user is sent a push notification when they log in to change their password, there's no way to know which multi-factor authentication push notification is tied to the password change, and which ones are from the attackers. This can be resolved by contacting the company's help desk or system administrator and having them reset the password on the account, so that the password the attacker has is no longer valid.

Users also need to be trained to never give out the multi-factor authentication code that is sent to them over text message, or that is shown in the multi-factor authentication application—ever. There is no valid time that the code should be given to anyone else, and anyone who asks for the code should be assumed to be an attacker who is trying to get the code for nefarious purposes.

Requiring the Use of Company Devices

Microsoft's Azure Active Directory includes a feature called Conditional Access. Using Conditional Access, we can extend multi-factor authentication to include additional features beyond just the requirement that the user uses MFA.

With Conditional Access you can define policies that require the user utilize specific operating systems, and whether their logins can come from a cell phone or a computer, and which operating system is in use on those devices, as shown in Figure 7-6.

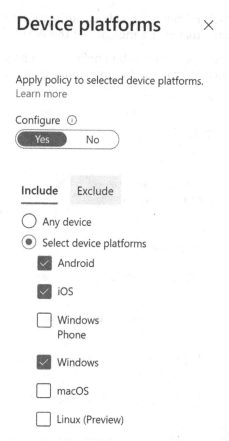

Figure 7-6. Platform selection of Azure Active Directory Conditional Access

Conditional Access gives the ability to require that the user is connecting via one of several authorized locations, such as the company's offices. By requiring that the user be at a known location, the user can be prevented from logging in from an unknown location. If logins need to be allowed from everywhere, the system administrators can configure different Conditional Access policies where logins from known locations require multi-factor authentication, while logins from unknown locations require that they are done using company computers.

There are a couple of different settings that can be configured within Conditional Access. Devices can be configured with specific software and specific settings through Microsoft Intune. When devices are correctly configured with Microsoft Intune, the computers are marked as "compliant."

Authentication requests can be configured to only be accepted if they are coming from computers that are joined to an Azure Active Directory device.

This prevents an attacker from being able to authenticate if they are trying to do so from a computer that isn't a member of the Active Directory domain.

The Conditional Access policies can be configured to require just one of the selected requirements, or all of the selected requirements, as shown in Figure 7-7.

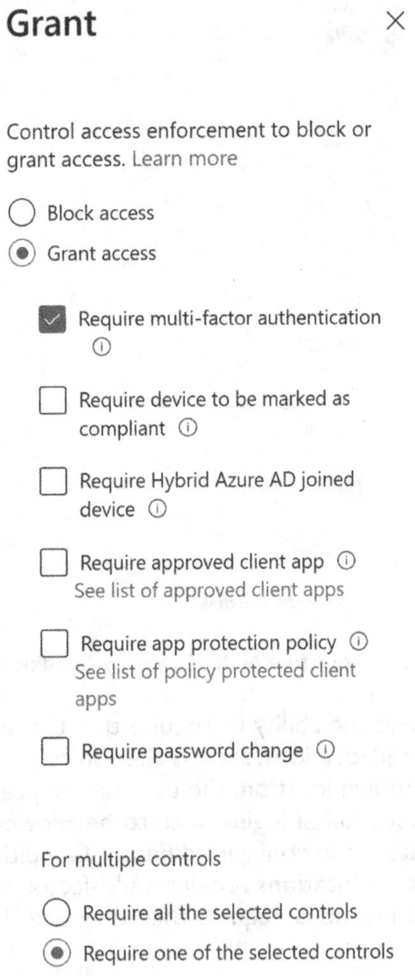

Grant   ×

Control access enforcement to block or grant access. Learn more

◯ Block access

◉ Grant access

☑ Require multi-factor authentication ⓘ

☐ Require device to be marked as compliant ⓘ

☐ Require Hybrid Azure AD joined device ⓘ

☐ Require approved client app ⓘ
See list of approved client apps

☐ Require app protection policy ⓘ
See list of policy protected client apps

☐ Require password change ⓘ

For multiple controls

◯ Require all the selected controls

◉ Require one of the selected controls

Figure 7-7. *Device authentication options in Conditional Access*

Applications used for authentication can be configured to require that the application being used is an approved application. This can be helpful if the attacker has built their own application to extract data from the user's account, as Azure Active Directory will reject the authentication request from the application.

Microsoft Azure Active Directory has a risk score associated with each user's account. This risk score is based on a user's logging in from locations that are physically far apart, when it would be impossible for the user to physically travel between those locations in the time between logins.

A perfect example of this if the user is based in California, and they log in and get their email, and then the user logs in to the Office 365 portal from a virtual machine in the East U.S. Microsoft Azure region. This would trigger the user's account to be flagged as high risk.

Note   This actually happened to me recently. I was logging in to the Visual Studio portal from my laptop, and then about five minutes later I logged in to the Visual Studio portal from a computer within the Azure West U.S. data center. As soon as that login happened, all of our company's Azure Active Directory environment were sent an email that my account was marked as high risk.

Policies can be configured to be used only by accounts marked as high risk, as shown in Figure 7-8.

Figure 7-8. Conditional Access policies configured to be used by users with medium or high risk

Policies can also be configured to require specific risk levels in order to log in. This prevents users who are considered high risk, as shown in Figure 7-9, from logging in. If the user is based in one country and the attacker is in another country, the user's account will be quickly flipped to high risk, which in the case shown in Figure 7-9 should prevent the attacker from being able to log in.

Figure 7-9. Conditional Access preventing sign-in for users that are high risk

Administrators can configure Azure Active Directory to require multi-factor authentication prompts, via Conditional Access, every X number of days, or via various other policies. The number of days for which a session is valid can be shortened or lengthened depending on the security posture of the environment and the tolerance of the users being prompted frequently for multi-factor authentication.

■ **Note** While users may complain about being frequently prompted for multi-factor authentication, a reasonable response from a security perspective is "too bad." While this response seems callous, security isn't about making the user's life easier; it's about protecting the computing environment.

Choose Platforms Carefully

In early 2022, there was a breach of the third-party multi-factor authentication provider Okta. This attack was dangerous, as Okta was handling the authentication for a wide variety of companies. The attackers were able to trigger multi-factor authentication prompts for users that gave them access to log in via the user's account, if the user approved the authentication request.

Multi-factor authentication shows that technical solutions to attacks need to be combined with user training to ensure that the environment is protected.

Zero-Trust Environments

Zero trust is a new concept in information technology security. The easiest way to understand the configuration of a zero-trust environment is to compare it to a more traditional network configuration.

In a traditional network configuration, such as the configurations discussed in Chapter 2 of this book, once a user gets onto the network, either by connecting via a virtual private network via the internet, or by being physically located in a company's office, they can connect to any service within the network they have access to, as shown in Figure 8-1. This moving from service to server, or server to server, is called moving laterally within the network. This is one of the techniques an attacker uses when they attack a network. They will compromise a single user, and then once the attacker has gotten into the company network, they will move laterally to other services, often using privilege escalation to increase their access.

© Denny Cherry 2022
D. Cherry, *Enterprise-Grade IT Security for Small and Medium Businesses*,
https://doi.org/10.1007/978-1-4842-8628-9_8

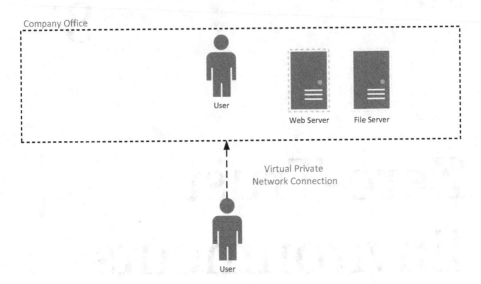

Figure 8-1. Traditional network, which allows for lateral movement

With a zero-trust network, this lateral movement isn't possible, as each service the user attempts to access requires two different authorizations: one for the user's account and one for the device, both of which are authorized by the zero-trust platform the company is using, as shown in Figure 8-2. If the user tries to get access to an application using an unknown device, their authentication request is denied. If a user tries to gain access to an application with their device and they have not been granted access to it, their authentication request is denied.

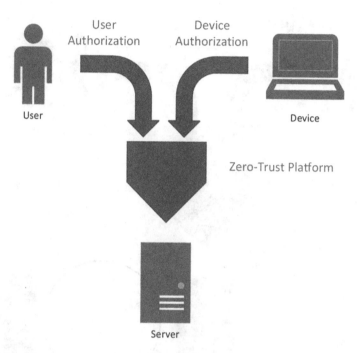

Figure 8-2. Access process when using a zero-trust platform

The big advantage of a zero-trust environment compared to a traditional platform configuration is that if the user attempts to move laterally from one server to another, they are denied, as shown in Figure 8-3.

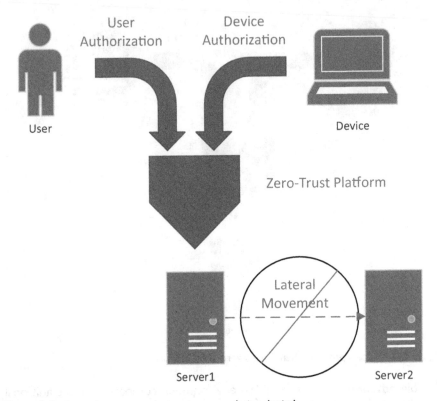

Figure 8-3. Lateral movement between servers being denied

For the user to get access to Server2, shown in Figure 8-3, the connection needs to go through the zero-trust platform again. If the user has access to Server2, and the connection is coming from the user's device, they can have access. If the user's account has been compromised and the connection to Server2 comes from Server1 instead of the user's device, the connection will be rejected as it isn't authorized.

While the concept of a zero-trust platform is pretty straightforward to conceptualize, the implementation can be quite a bit more difficult. Because of this, many companies (and the system administrators who manage the environments at those companies) shy away from these environments.

■ **Note**   While any company can deploy a zero-trust environment, the salary requirements of system administrators who have experience with zero-trust networks are going to be higher than those of system administrators who aren't familiar with zero-trust environments.

One of the side effects of having a zero-trust environment is that the platform can generate a huge amount of data, as every connection request, whether approved or denied, is logged. This logging has a few perks the company can take advantage of, however.

The first perk is that when a person makes unusual connection attempts, those connection attempts can be found. For example, if an employee normally uses the system from 9 a.m. to 6 p.m. Monday through Friday from Denver, Colorado (USA), and suddenly starts attempting to access the system at 10 a.m. from China, just hours after they used the system from Denver, Colorado, we can assume that the user's account has been compromised.

Machine learning and artificial intelligence techniques can be used to review the data in real time so that alerts about the potential breach can be raised to staff in real time, or near real time. While these machine learning and artificial intelligence platforms can be expensive to deploy on-premises, building these solutions in the cloud can be very cost effective.

With machine learning processing the data in real time, the system can learn the user's normal usage patterns. Once the machine learning system has done so, it will be able to identify anomalies and then can contact the system administrators via email, text message, Microsoft Teams, Slack, etc. to alert them.

These usage patterns can also be used by the zero-trust platforms to adapt the approval process based on the risk that the user's login has. When a user's account is being used normally their risk level would be set for "None," as their login has no risk associated with it. If the user's account authenticates successfully from another location, and it isn't possible to physically travel that far in the amount of time that has passed, the user's risk profile can be switched to "High," with extra authentication required, or access requests rejected.

Note This risk-assessment change can be intentionally triggered by using virtual machines in various cloud regions. A test account was able to trigger this by using an Azure Active Directory account to log in to a Microsoft service from a virtual machine hosted in Microsoft Azure's West U.S. Region, and then connecting to another machine hosted in Microsoft Azure's East U.S. Region.

While West U.S. is in central California, East U.S. is in Virginia. Normally, these sites would be a six-hour flight apart, but the test login made this trip in about 30 seconds, as that was the amount of time between logins. Thankfully this was just a test, but this triggered the Azure Active Directory platform to switch the test account from having a risk profile of "None" to a risk profile of "High."

If desired, Azure Active Directory could be configured to reject access to services when the account has a risk profile set to "High."

The second advantage of zero-trust environments is that every request attempt is logged. This gives the company the ability to see when an attempt was made to breach the network, if the request was successful or rejected, and what systems the attacker tried to breach. This information can be useful, and possibly needed by law enforcement if a successful breach is detected.

What Can Be Secured Using a Zero-Trust Environment?

Zero-trust platforms can be used to secure any system that is hosted within an on-premises data center, or that is hosted in a cloud platform so long as the application is hosted within an Infrastructure as a Service (IaaS) configuration. Applications that use Platform as a Service (PaaS) offerings, such as Azure SQL DB or Amazon's AWS Route 53, can't typically be configured for zero trust. There are ways to work around some of these limitations. Some Software as a Service (SaaS) applications can be configured to work with zero-trust environments, while others cannot. It is up to the SaaS provider as to whether they support the zero-trust configuration or not.

When zero trust was first introduced, the only communication that it protected was users talking to applications. But applications talking to other applications over application programming interfaces (APIs) wasn't included. Several different zero-trust providers have included API-to-API communications as a part of their zero-trust platforms, which allows for any design holes opened because of the API-to-API communications be to closed and this communication secured.

With this extra level of protection, companies that have deployed zero-trust environments can close a security hole that was left open by the initial implementations of zero-trust networking. In addition to allowing services within the enterprise to securely communicate within the enterprise, this also allows external services such as IOT devices to communicate securely within the management systems of those devices. This gives the advantage that only devices that have the zero-trust networking software installed and configured are able to connect to the management systems, instead of allowing the management systems to be available on the public internet and accessible to bad actors who want to access them.

Just In Time Access

Along with zero-trust networks is the concept of Just In Time (JIT) access. The concept is that employees get access to systems for a small period of time so that they can perform the process they need to complete.

When using a Just In Time process, the employee requests an elevation of their own permissions. There can be an approval process to increase the employee's access, or the approval process can be automatic. In either case, the request is logged. The system that handles the granting of the JIT is typically going to be protected, preferably by multi-factor authentication.

Just In Time access can be configured with whatever granularity is needed to support the business needs. Often, companies will set administrative rights to systems behind Just In Time access. In this fashion, no user has administrative rights to the system under normal circumstances. In the event that an administrator needs to perform some management functions on the system, that user can use the JIT system to elevate their permissions on the system temporarily. After just a few seconds, the administrator will have administrative rights on the system for a short period of time, typically between one and eight hours.

The benefit of the JIT process is that there is no way to configure additional administrative access time for the systems. Access can only be granted through the Just In Time system. There are a variety of systems that fill the role of the Just In Time system. One popular and easy-to-configure system is available through the Microsoft Azure platform and is called Privileged Identity Management (PIM).

With Privileged Identity Management you can configure Just In Time access for management of the Azure infrastructure as well as dozens of other predefined rights within the Microsoft Azure and Office 365 environments. Additionally, groups can be configured that give rights, and access to be members of these groups can be handled by the PIM system.

This gives the company the greatest level of flexibility, as these groups are Azure Active Directory groups and can be configured to grant any sort of needed access to systems within the company.

By protecting administrative rights behind a Just In Time system, the computer systems are protected from an attacker who gets access to an administrative account. This assumes that the Just In Time system is protected by either a multi-factor authentication system or by having a Just In Time process in place that requires approvals to gain the needed access.

If the system is protected by multi-factor authentication, an attacker wouldn't have access to the mobile device of the employee. If approvals are required, the person who approves the access would need to verify that the employee was the one who requested the access, and why they need the access.

Conditional Access

Additional protection can be built around the concept of conditional access. With conditional access specific rules around authentication can be built. These rules can include the employee's being in a known location, such as an office, or not.

The conditional access method that is used will be one provided by the authentication provider that is used for web-based authentication. An example of this is the Azure Conditional Access feature of Microsoft Azure.

With Azure Conditional Access you can select where the user needs to be when multi-factor authentication is used, as well as what kind of authentication is supported. You can configure the conditional access policy so that logins can only be done from company-managed computers, or from mobile devices registered with and managed by the company. This gives the company protection from people attempting to log in from computers that aren't managed by the company, which includes both employees and attackers who have valid credentials.

In addition to these requirements, the login risk profile of the account can be taken into account. As an example, accounts that have a high risk profile can be configured to have a more strict security posture than accounts that don't have a high risk profile.

Policy Conditions

Using the various security rules available, accounts that are used by employees who travel, or who use computers (or virtual machines) in multiple physical locations, can have higher authentication requirements than users who only use their accounts from within the company's facilities. When configuring Conditional Access policies, different policies can be configured for a variety of conditions. These include the following:

- User's Risk Profile
- Current Sign-in Risk
- Device Operating System
- User's Location
- Application Login Method
- Device Metadata

Once the policy is configured with the correct filters, login can be allowed or denied based on the use of multi-factor authentication, if the device is managed by the company through Azure Active Directory, or if the device is listed as compliant within Azure Active Directory. Policies can also be configured to allow logins for approved client applications (currently Microsoft applications).

The policies defined within Conditional Access are set up to be easy to understand and easy to configure with just a few checkboxes.

User's Risk Profile

User risk profiles within Azure Active Directory are configured automatically based on the physical locations where the account is logged in to. When an account logs in from different physical locations and the time between these logins is less than the amount of time needed to travel between these locations, the user risk profile is increased. By default, all users are configured for a "Low" risk profile, and that profile is increased when logins from different cities or countries within too short of a time period occur.

The physical location of the user's device is known based on the public internet protocol (IP) address of the device. The public IP address of a device is registered to a specific location, typically a country or city. While companies that own large blocks of public IP addresses can move those IP addresses from one country to another, this does not happen frequently, and cannot be done by an individual.

Note   Around 2019, Microsoft caused a little bit of havoc with identifying locations as they moved a large block of IP addresses from their Azure region in Brazil to one of the Azure regions in the United States. This caused virtual machines with IP addresses in that block to appear to be in Brazil when getting their location information until Microsoft was able to change the registry on the virtual machines.

The physical location of the device can also be masked by the user by using a virtual private network (VPN), as this allows all the network traffic to be sent through the VPN, making the public IP address of the device appear as the VPN's public IP address, not the public IP address of the device itself. This can be used both by bad actors as well as by company employees who need to access websites that are restricted by geographic region.

Note   As a small-business owner, I have to make use of this trick when traveling outside of the United States of America. As part of our company's employment package, we offer a 401k retirement account, like most companies in the United States do. Managing this account can only be done from the United States. After each payroll is run, I have to upload the payroll information to the retirement company's website.

The company that manages the retirement accounts does not work from outside the United States, which makes sense as their services are only available in the United States. Because of this restriction, when I travel to other countries I have to connect to a virtual private network based in the United States in order to connect to this website and upload the needed information.

When a Conditional Access policy is configured based on the user's risk, a set of simple checkboxes is provided, as shown in Figure 8-4.

Figure 8-4. User risk options within Microsoft's Azure Active Directory Conditional Access policy

Current Sign-in Risk

The current sign-in risk is based on the same location information as the user's risk assessment discussed in the previous section. The difference between the two is that a user's account might have a low risk assignment, while the current sign-in attempt might be considered high risk.

When the user's current login attempt is done from the same public IP address as their prior logins, the risk profile as the current sign-in will be "Low" or "None."

When the user's current login attempt is done from a different country than the prior login attempts, the current sign-in risk will be elevated. When the current login attempt is from another country than the prior logins for the account, and the amount of time that has passed from the previous login to the current login is less than the amount of time needed to travel between the cities, then the current sign-in risk will be elevated, potentially up to "High."

Sign-ins that are at risk should always be configured to require multi-factor authentication, if not limited to company devices. User sign-in risk is configured within a conditional policy with checkboxes, allowing the policy to be easily configured, as shown in Figure 8-5.

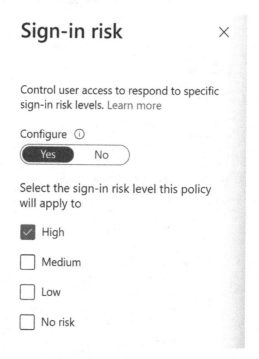

Figure 8-5. Sign-in risk configuration within Microsoft's Azure Active Directory Conditional Access

Device Operating System

The Conditional Access policy can be applied to any device or to specific operating systems, as shown in Figure 8-6.

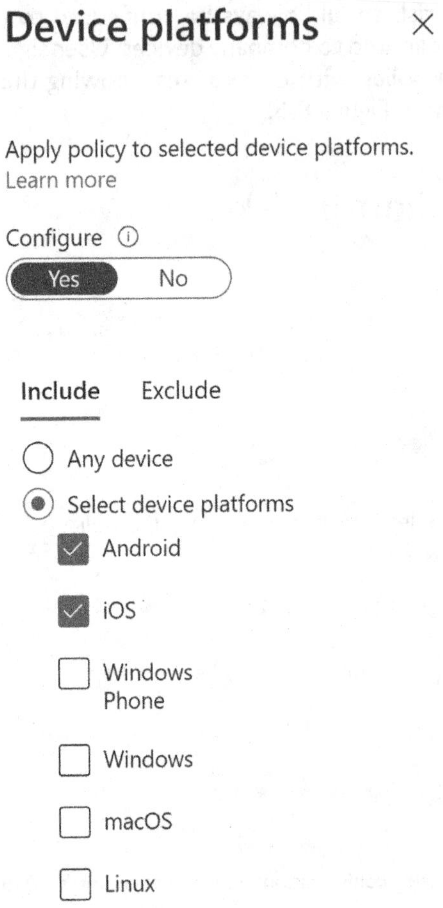

Device platforms   ×

Apply policy to selected device platforms.
Learn more

Configure ⓘ

(**Yes**   No)

Include   Exclude

◯ Any device

⦿ Select device platforms

☑ Android

☑ iOS

☐ Windows
Phone

☐ Windows

☐ macOS

☐ Linux

Figure 8-6. Device platform selection within Microsoft's Azure Active Directory Conditional Access

This allows for different Conditional Access policies to be used for different operating systems. If, for example, the company only uses Windows computers and users only own Android and iOS devices, then a Conditional Access policy could be configured that prevents logins from Linux and macOS devices as well as Windows phones.

Devices can either be included in the policy, or be specifically excluded from the policy as needed.

Locations

As part of setting up a Conditional Access policy, locations can be configured. The policy can be configured to be enabled for specific locations, or it can be enabled for everyone, with specific locations such as the company's office being excluded from the policy, as shown in Figure 8-7. When we exclude a location from a policy we are not saying that the location is excluded from access, but rather that users who authenticate from the location are not required to use MFA.

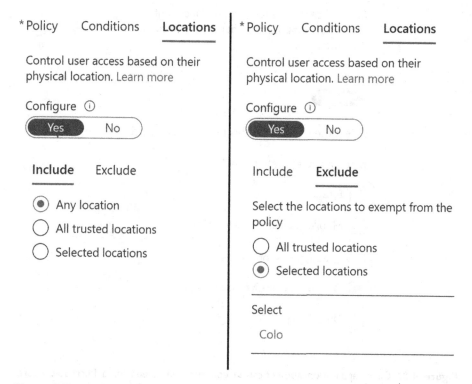

Figure 8-7. Location configuration within a Microsoft Azure Active Directory Conditional Access policy

Application Login Method

Microsoft allows for two different login methods, depending on the application being used to log in. The two methods are called *legacy authentication* and *modern authentication*. Older applications such as Outlook 2003 and other applications that use the Exchange ActiveSync client, as well as other older applications, would use legacy authentication. Modern authentication clients are applications such as modern versions of Microsoft Office, as well as web-based logins.

Logins that match the configured authentication protocols will have the Conditional Access policy applied to them. This setting is very useful if you want to block authentication requests that come from legacy authentication clients. This configuration is shown in Figure 8-8.

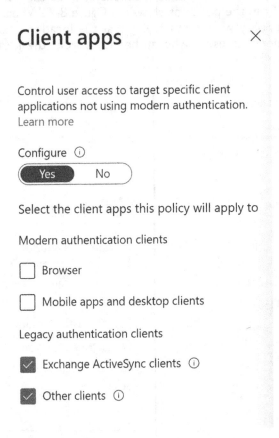

Figure 8-8. Client application authentication configuration screen for a Microsoft Azure Active Directory Contained Access policy

Device Metadata

The most complex configuration for a Conditional Access policy allows for device configuration. With the device-filtering rules, the policy can be configured to apply to a specific device, or to a set of devices based on operating system or device compliance as reported by Microsoft Intune, as shown in Figure 8-9.

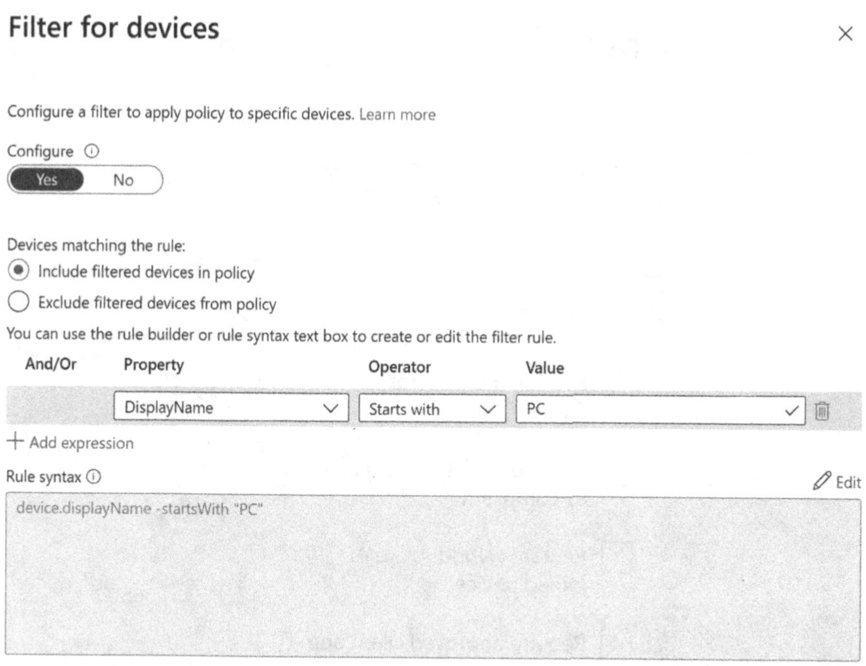

Filter for devices ✕

Configure a filter to apply policy to specific devices. Learn more

Configure ⓘ

[**Yes** | No]

Devices matching the rule:
◉ Include filtered devices in policy
◯ Exclude filtered devices from policy

You can use the rule builder or rule syntax text box to create or edit the filter rule.

And/Or	Property	Operator	Value
	DisplayName ⌄	Starts with ⌄	PC ✓ 🗑

╋ Add expression

Rule syntax ⓘ   ✎ Edit

```
device.displayName -startsWith "PC"
```

Figure 8-9. Device filter for a Microsoft Azure Active Directory Conditional Access policy using the device's name

The Property selection menu on the device filter screen is extremely flexible, allowing the policy to be applied, with a wide variety of options available. The policy can be configured to apply to devices that match the policy filter, or those that do not match the policy filter.

Access Controls

Azure Active Directory policies can be configured to block authentication requests, or to grant the authentication request, assuming that the enabled authentication rules are met. The available rules are shown in Figure 8-10.

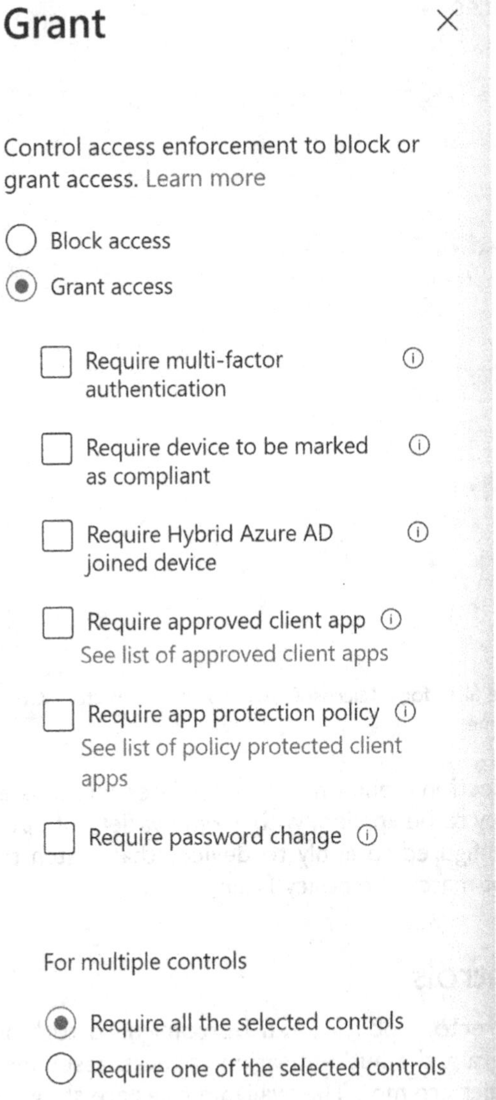

Grant   ✕

Control access enforcement to block or grant access. Learn more

○ Block access

◉ Grant access

   ☐ Require multi-factor   ⓘ
       authentication

   ☐ Require device to be marked ⓘ
       as compliant

   ☐ Require Hybrid Azure AD   ⓘ
       joined device

   ☐ Require approved client app ⓘ
       See list of approved client apps

   ☐ Require app protection policy ⓘ
       See list of policy protected client
       apps

   ☐ Require password change ⓘ

For multiple controls

◉ Require all the selected controls

○ Require one of the selected controls

Figure 8-10. Available rules for an authentication request to be granted by Microsoft's Azure Active Directory Conditional Access

If the company wishes to block login attempts classified as high risk, this would be done by setting the Sign-in risk, shown in Figure 8-5, to "High," setting the policy to apply to all device platforms (Figure 8-6), and setting the settings for device operating system, location, and the device filter to "not configured," with the access panel, shown in Figure 8-10, set to "blocked."

Tip   When configuring a Conditional Access policy, the person configuring the policy should configure their account to be exempt from the policy while testing the policy. The policy can then be tested using a test account. This way if there is a problem with the settings of the policy it is not possible to lock yourself out.

If all accounts are blocked by a Conditional Access policy, Microsoft Support will need to be contacted in order to remove the policy to enable access to the system again.

While it is difficult to lock yourself out of the Azure platform, it is possible.

Policy Status

When configuring of the Conditional Access policy is complete, the policy needs to be enabled. By default, policies will be in "Report-only" mode, where the Microsoft Azure Active Directory platform will authenticate users as normal, but log if the policy would have been effected. If the policy status is set to "On," then the policy is in effect. Policies set to "Off" will not be applied.

The People

The Weakest Security Link—People

Generally speaking, the weakest link in information technology security isn't how the devices are configured or what solutions have been configured. The weakest link is the general office staff. The company can put hundreds of thousands of dollars into protecting the computing environment, but that is no match for Fred in customer service who finds a USB thumb drive on the ground in the parking lot and plugs it into their company computer to see what's on it.

© Denny Cherry 2022
D. Cherry, *Enterprise-Grade IT Security for Small and Medium Businesses*,
https://doi.org/10.1007/978-1-4842-8628-9_9

USB can be a tricky platform. As users we want everything that we plug into a USB port to just work, which includes USB thumb drives, cell phones, portal hard drives, etc. To work, the device has to be able to install whatever drivers are needed to function. These drivers can be compromised so that when the device is plugged into the computer, the compromised software is then installed on the computer.

Why Workers Are the Weakest Link

While technology solutions can be used to solve a lot of information technology security–related issues, they can't solve all of them. Sadly, companies can spend as much money as they want on technology solutions, but if the users' ability to do things that will hurt the company isn't limited, the users will find a way to end up hurting the company.

USB

The USB ports on the company's computers (and the users that insert devices into them) can be a massive security risk for companies. This is because by default Windows will mount the thumb drive and run the application that's on the drive. If there is a virus on the device, that virus will be opened and run, infecting the user's computer, and potentially any other devices on the network to which the virus is able to connect. There are settings within Windows that can prevent the automatic running of the software on the device; however, any drivers needed by the device will have to be installed manually.

A shockingly effective attack vector is for an attacker to purchase 50 small USB drives, infecting each of them with a virus that exfiltrates data from the company's computers to the attacker via the internet. Instead of breaking into the company's offices and risking identification by any security cameras the company has in place, the attacker can simply spread the USB drives around the parking lot of the office. Odds are that one of the USB drives will be picked up by an employee, and odds are they will plug the USB drive into their office computer. If none of the drives are plugged in, the attacker can just try again.

It doesn't even require putting the drives in the parking lot, which may or may not have security cameras. In cities like New York City, the USB drives could be simply "dropped" on the subway system. Given the large number of people who take the New York City subway each day, the odds of someone picking up the USB drives is high, and by using a platform like the subway the attacker would possibly get access to and infect multiple companies. The odds of being identified as the person who dropped the USB drives are basically zero.

To prevent these sorts of attacks, there's a few different approaches that companies can take. There's software solutions, which can be used to prevent people from using USB ports. There's Active Directory settings, which can prevent the USB ports from opening applications on the USB drives. Some companies take the approach of disabling the USB ports in the computers' BIOS settings. Some people take a slightly more low-tech approach to disabling the USB ports by putting super glue in the USB ports. Super glue doesn't conduct electricity once it's dry, and it dries quickly. By filling the USB ports with glue, they are disabled from functioning and there's no way for the user to remove the glue from the port.

Email

Email attacks are a major avenue for an attacker to get into a computer network. Users get emails all day long, and some users will click on any attachment that they receive, as they assume that the email received is safe. However, that isn't always the case.

Users need to assume that every attachment that comes in is an attack. Some of the emails that are attack attempts are easy to identify, and some aren't. The email in Figure 9-1 can be fairly easily identified as a junk email.

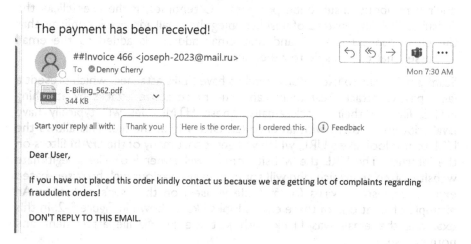

Figure 9-1. SPAM email that can be identified easily

The first way to notice that the email shown in Figure 9-1 is SPAM is the return email address. I can guarantee you that my company has not purchased any services from anyone using a mail.ru email address. You'll also notice that the name of the email is Invoice 466, while the invoice attached is #562.

It is possible to embed a virus within a PDF file, so opening the file would start the attack on the company's computer environment. In some cases, the attacker is waiting for an email back from the people to whom the email was sent. The expectation is that people will email them back saying that the user never ordered the product, at which point the attacker can email the user and attempt to get them to give them a credit card to receive the supposed refund. However, no refund would be given; instead, the attacker would charge the credit card and run the credit card as high as possible.

The number of scam emails that a person gets can number in the hundreds or thousands per day. The longer a person's email address stays active, the more junk email the person is going to get.

■ **Note**   Personally, I have an email address that is 15 years old at this point. Because of this, the email address easily gets hundreds of junk emails a day. Thankfully, most of them are caught by the Office 365 security filtering used by my email address.

As an email address is added to various junk email lists that are traded and sold among spammers, the email address gets added to more and more lists. Clicking "unsubscribe" links doesn't do any good, as spammers and scammers don't care about unsubscribe processes. Oftentimes, if the user clicks the "unsubscribe" link, instead of unsubscribing the email address, it confirms that the email address is valid, and that email address is added to the email addresses that can be sold to other scammers.

Scam emails sent to users don't need to have PDFs attached, which present a fairly passive attack. Scammers can issue more active attacks by attaching HTML files to their attack emails. These HTML files will typically have JavaScript inside them with an encoded URL within the file. This allows the URL to not look like a URL, which will get it past many of the SPAM filters on the internet. The URL the website opens will either look like a legitimate website, often an invoice, and will sometimes use various web browser–based exploits to install a virus (or multiple viruses) on the user's computer. An example of what one of these emails looks like is shown in Figure 9-2. In this example, the email was blank with just the HTML file attachment and nothing else.

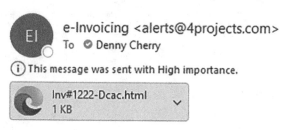

PO Confirmation for Inv #9389 April 5, 2022

EI   e-Invoicing <alerts@4projects.com>
To ✓ Denny Cherry

ⓘ This message was sent with High importance.

Inv#1222-Dcac.html
1 KB

Figure 9-2. Scam email with an "invoice" attached

Personalized Attacks

Attacks via email can be broad, where the same email message is sent to thousands or tens of thousands of people. Attacks can also be more personalized, sometimes much more personalized. Email attacks that go to a large number of people are called phishing (fishing) attacks. Email attacks sent to a small group of people, or even a single person, are called spear-phishing attacks. These attacks can be incredibly personal and can use personal information to make the emails look more legitimate.

The CEO of a former client of mine was once purchasing an item from a friend, who was an executive of another company. They had been talking about the purchase and finished arranging the details, including the purchase price, via email. Shortly after they finalized the details, the CEO received an email that appeared to be a request for a wire transfer with a link that appeared to be for a wire transfer service.

The link to the wire transfer was actually to a compromised website that was collecting usernames and passwords, and it looked just like the Microsoft authentication website. The CEO attempted to log in to the website, and they were given a password failure message, which is the usual modus operandi for websites that are capturing usernames and passwords. Thankfully the company had protected all employee accounts with multi-factor authentication.

To the CEO's credit, as soon as he hit Enter he realized what he had done, and we contacted the IT department, which immediately changed his password and checked his computer for viruses through a third-party firm. Before the device was given back to the user, the device was imaged, just to be safe.

The first change that was made to better secure the company's accounts was to the Microsoft Azure Active Directory login screen. By default, the screen has a blank background, as shown in Figure 9-3. This background can be changed to any graphic that the company wants—to a generic image or a graphic that has the company logo.

Figure 9-3. The default login screen for Azure Active Directory

By changing the background from the default grey background to a custom image, as soon as the user enters their email address and clicks Next, the background is changed to show the image. The user can use this change to ensure that they are on the legitimate Azure Active Directory website instead of a third-party site. Employees should be told that the image is legitimate, and that if the password screen doesn't show the custom image, then the website should be closed and reported to the information technology team.

One of the oldest, most common, and sadly most successful scams out there involves emails promising to give you money, either from a lottery, from a soldier who has "found" money (these were very popular during the United States' war in Iraq), from a banker who has money they need to get out of the country that they claim to be in (often from a deceased person), or from the classic Nigerian prince who needs to get money out of Nigeria for some reason or another.

These email scams have not slowed down, really at all. Just recently, I received another one (it was caught by the junk-mail filter in Office 365), which you can see in Figure 9-4.

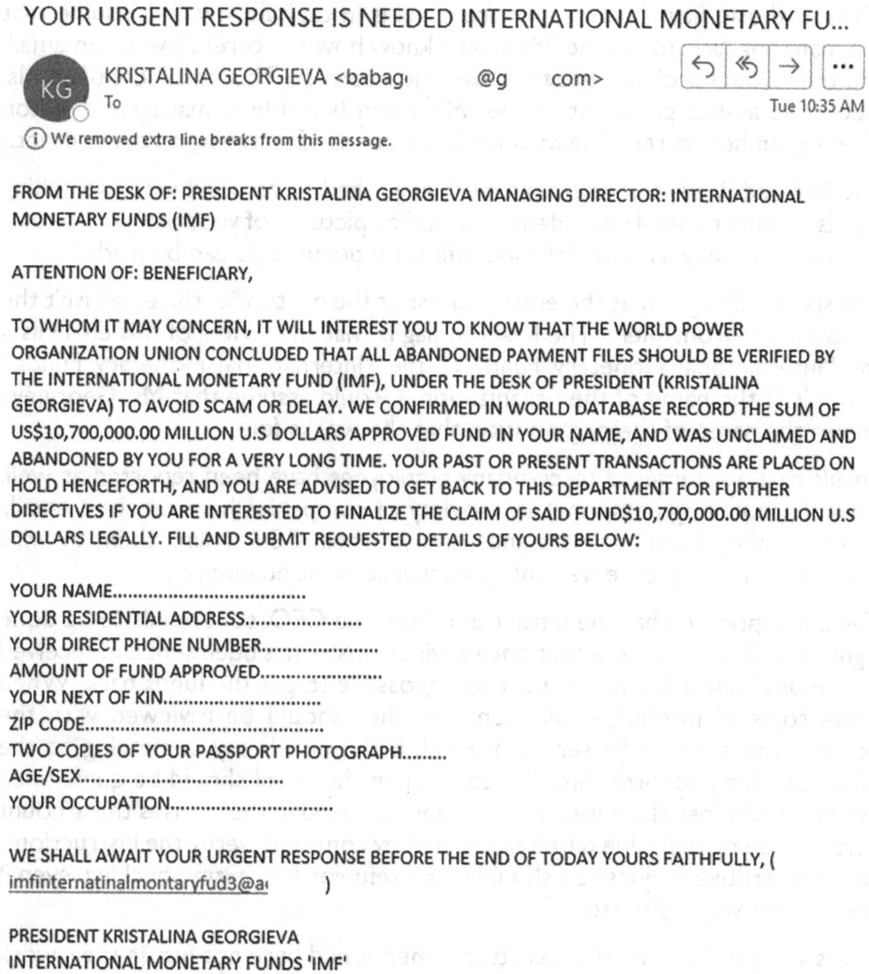

YOUR URGENT RESPONSE IS NEEDED INTERNATIONAL MONETARY FU...

KG KRISTALINA GEORGIEVA <babag   @g   com>   ↶ ↞ → ···
To   Tue 10:35 AM

ⓘ We removed extra line breaks from this message.

FROM THE DESK OF: PRESIDENT KRISTALINA GEORGIEVA MANAGING DIRECTOR: INTERNATIONAL
MONETARY FUNDS (IMF)

ATTENTION OF: BENEFICIARY,

TO WHOM IT MAY CONCERN, IT WILL INTEREST YOU TO KNOW THAT THE WORLD POWER
ORGANIZATION UNION CONCLUDED THAT ALL ABANDONED PAYMENT FILES SHOULD BE VERIFIED BY
THE INTERNATIONAL MONETARY FUND (IMF), UNDER THE DESK OF PRESIDENT (KRISTALINA
GEORGIEVA) TO AVOID SCAM OR DELAY. WE CONFIRMED IN WORLD DATABASE RECORD THE SUM OF
US$10,700,000.00 MILLION U.S DOLLARS APPROVED FUND IN YOUR NAME, AND WAS UNCLAIMED AND
ABANDONED BY YOU FOR A VERY LONG TIME. YOUR PAST OR PRESENT TRANSACTIONS ARE PLACED ON
HOLD HENCEFORTH, AND YOU ARE ADVISED TO GET BACK TO THIS DEPARTMENT FOR FURTHER
DIRECTIVES IF YOU ARE INTERESTED TO FINALIZE THE CLAIM OF SAID FUND$10,700,000.00 MILLION U.S
DOLLARS LEGALLY. FILL AND SUBMIT REQUESTED DETAILS OF YOURS BELOW:

YOUR NAME.....................................
YOUR RESIDENTIAL ADDRESS.......................
YOUR DIRECT PHONE NUMBER........................
AMOUNT OF FUND APPROVED.........................
YOUR NEXT OF KIN..............................
ZIP CODE......................................
TWO COPIES OF YOUR PASSPORT PHOTOGRAPH.........
AGE/SEX.......................................
YOUR OCCUPATION...............................

WE SHALL AWAIT YOUR URGENT RESPONSE BEFORE THE END OF TODAY YOURS FAITHFULLY, (
imfinternatinalmontaryfud3@a   )

PRESIDENT KRISTALINA GEORGIEVA
INTERNATIONAL MONETARY FUNDS 'IMF'

Figure 9-4. Scam email example

There are several red flags that should immediately create pause in anyone
who receives an email like this. The first is that the "To" field is blank. This is
because the scammer just sends out a single email with several hundred
people in the "BCC" field.

Second, the "from" email address isn't even close to the name that is shown.
The name is Kristalina Georgieva (this is the name of the current managing
director), but the email address starts with "babag." The third red flag is that
the email is from a generic free email service. Official emails from government
or businesspeople will come from their company's or agency's official email
address—not from a generic free email service.

The fourth red flag is that the entire email is in capitals. I would assume that the managing director of the IMF would know how to correctly write an email, and they would probably get their own title correct. This email identified Ms. Georgieva as the president of the IMF, when her title is managing director. (Finding out her correct title took me five seconds of searching on the internet.)

The fifth red flag is that the reader is being asked to respond with everything that is needed to steal your identity, including pictures of your passport photo, so that, I can only assume, fake identification documents can be made.

The sixth red flag is that the email address at the bottom of the email isn't the same as the "from" field. The final red flag is that the writer of this email lists the "International Monetary Fund" as the "International Monetary Funds," which isn't the name of the organization. I would assume that Ms. Georgieva knows the name of the organization that she works for.

Emails that are targeted to company employees have been reported as well. Several accounting personnel at a variety of companies have received emails that have the "from" address and name of their CEO telling them to wire transfer money to some new international account number.

The assumption is that the email came from the CEO, so it needs to be done right away. The problem is that once a wire transfer has been sent and received by the destination bank, it is next to impossible to get the funds back. When these sorts of internal emails come in, they should be reviewed with the person who supposedly sent the email. If the emails say something to the effect of "don't confirm this, just do it" then the email should be questioned even more, before the wire transfer is sent off. And in these cases the account person is doing their due diligence when they come and verify the instructions, so the executive in question should be grateful for this extra checking, even if the request was legitimate.

Users will get the sort of email attacks mentioned here not just in their work email, but in their personal email as well. While it might not seem like a personal email asking an employee for their personal banking information is a company problem, it can become one.

Assume that the employee responds to a scam email where they need to send a small guaranteed amount of money to a scammer before the scammer can send them millions of dollars.[1] The goal of these scammers is to financially drain the victim, taking everything from them that they can. This can lead to the employee's not being able to pay their rent, mortgage, car loan, or other bills, and can lead the employee to do something they might not normally do, such as "borrow" money from the company. While the attacker may have

---

[1] The FBI and the Internet Crime Complaint Center (IC3) estimated in their 2017 Internet Crime Report that over $57 million was taken from crime victims as fees for collecting larger sums. More information is available from https://www.egits4smb.com/go/ic3.

been able to convince them that this is just borrowing, the authorities will probably call this embezzling instead.

Cell Phone Cameras

The unfortunate reality is that employees are often the avenue by which data in a company gets breached. Employees are trusted to have access to large amounts of confidential data.

Even when the company blocks access to email customer data (there are a variety of tools that will read through people's emails and ensure that there are no Social Security numbers, tax numbers, account numbers, etc. within the email), but there's one way that a nefarious employee could still gather customer information, and that is by taking a picture of the information on their computer screen with their cell phone.

In modern times, every cell phone has a camera built into it. Companies can't expect employees to leave their cell phones at home or in their car.[2] Emergency phone calls come in from their kids, their significant other, or other family members all the time. The company can't be the reason that these emergency calls aren't answered. Having access to your cell phone is just a standard way of life at this point.

Because of this, we need to look even more at the concept of least privilege (discussed later in this chapter), as well as at auditing access to personal information such as addresses, credit card numbers, etc. This way, whenever this information is viewed, it is logged somewhere in the system. Later, if a person's information is accessed in a breach, the company can ensure that they were not the cause of the breach. If there is a possibility that an employee was accessing personal information that they shouldn't have been accessing, the appropriate action can be taken.

Text Messages

Text messages on the user's mobile device (including Discord, What's App, Instagram, etc.) are another way that users can attempt to attack or scam users. In Figure 9-5, the text message sent attempts to get users' banking credentials.

---

[2] Some companies, especially those that do high-security government work, require their employees to keep their devices outside of the secure area of their office.

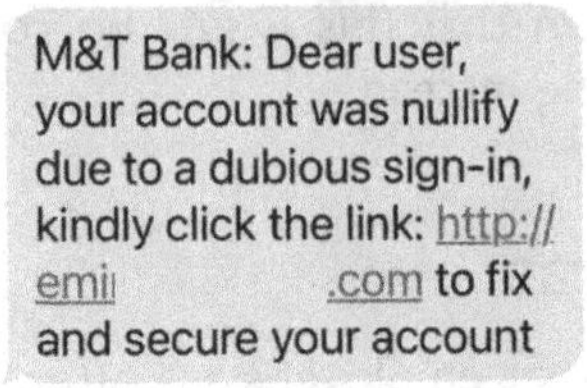

> M&T Bank: Dear user, your account was nullify due to a dubious sign-in, kindly click the link: http:// emii   .com to fix and secure your account

Figure 9-5. Scam text message

The first thing to know about the text message is that it was sent to a user who isn't a customer of M&T Bank. The first hint that this isn't from M&T Bank is that the website that is in the text message isn't M&T's website. The actual website for M&T is www.mtb.com, not something starting with an "e." Going to the URL in the text message takes you to a website that looks very legitimate, other than the URL's being wrong. The fake login screen is shown in Figure 9-6, while the real login screen is shown in Figure 9-7.

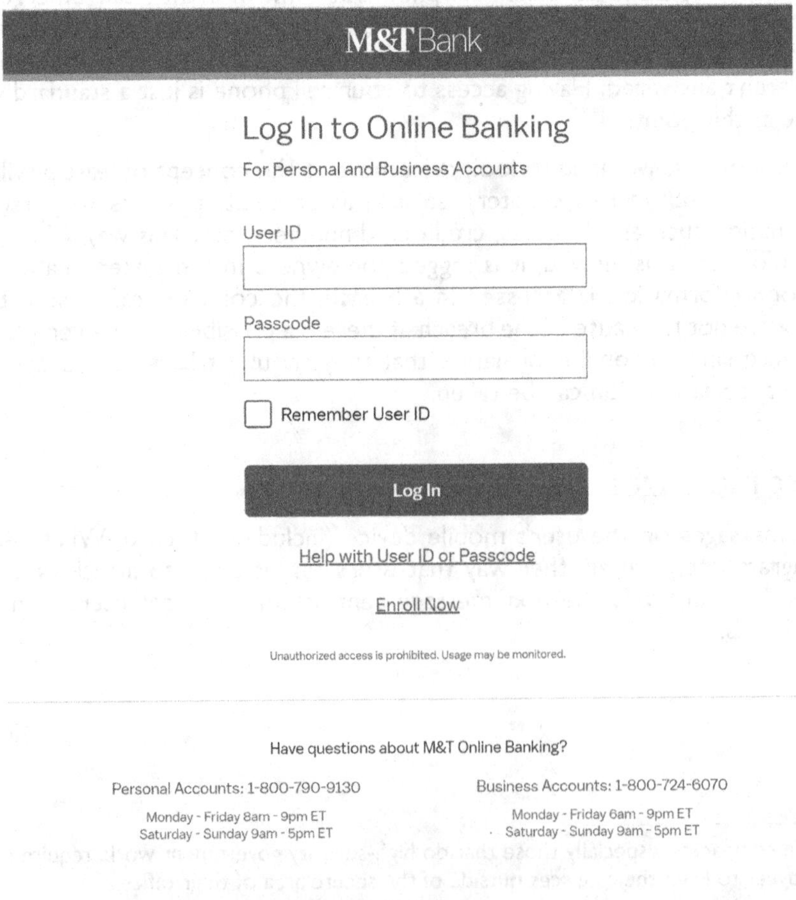

M&T Bank

Log In to Online Banking

For Personal and Business Accounts

User ID

Passcode

☐ Remember User ID

    Log In

Help with User ID or Passcode

Enroll Now

Unauthorized access is prohibited. Usage may be monitored.

Have questions about M&T Online Banking?

Personal Accounts: 1-800-790-9130

Business Accounts: 1-800-724-6070

Monday - Friday 8am - 9pm ET
Saturday - Sunday 9am - 5pm ET

Monday - Friday 6am - 9pm ET
Saturday - Sunday 9am - 5pm ET

Figure 9-6. Fake version of the M&T Bank login screen

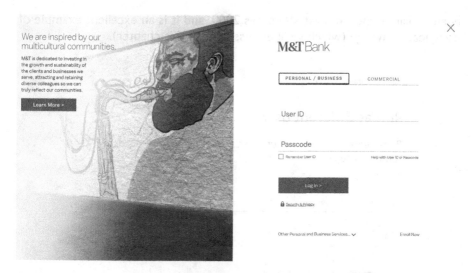

Figure 9-7. Real version of the M&T Bank login screen

As you can see in Figure 9-6, the login screen looks like it could be a legitimate login screen, if you weren't familiar with the actual login screen from Figure 9-7. The hope of the scammer is that the user won't notice that the website doesn't match the official website.

While this example is for a public website, more-targeted text messages could be sent to staff members with internal website names, or even the company's name and a totally fake-looking URL.

Administrative Rights on Computers

Users should not have administrative rights to their computers. While this is a strong stance, it will help prevent configuration issues on their computers, and will prevent the installation of rogue software that the user has downloaded.

Users that do need to have administrative rights to their computer should do so via a second account, with their normal account having no special access to their computer or to the network. The second account, often called an *admin account*, does have administrative rights to the computer, and when needed the user can start an application as that additional account that has administrative rights.

While some people will complain that this presents too much of a barrier for them to effectively work (this is the typical excuse), it is simply a matter of right-clicking on the application, selecting the "Run as administrator" option, and then entering your credentials, as shown in Figure 9-8. This option has been available since at least Windows 2000, and it is an excellent example of using least privilege (which we'll discuss later in this chapter).

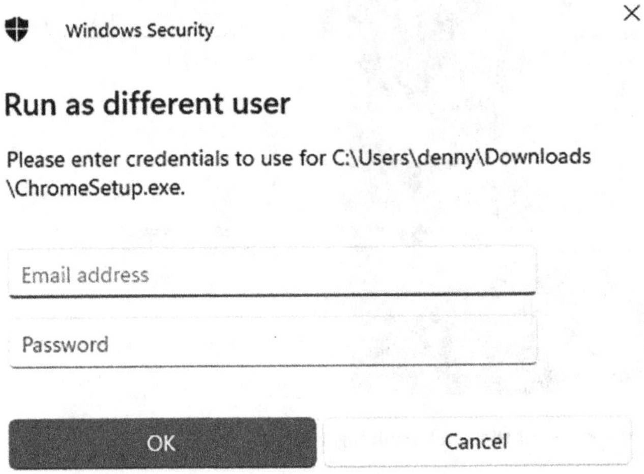

Windows Security   ✕

Run as different user

Please enter credentials to use for C:\Users\denny\Downloads
\ChromeSetup.exe.

Email address

Password

OK	Cancel

Figure 9-8. Screen allowing the Chrome installer to be run as a different Windows account in the Microsoft Windows operating system

By limiting what software can be run on the computer, and what software can be installed on the computer, we can eliminate a large number of potential threats to the company's environment.

Why Workers Need Regular Security Training

Everyone in the company—from the person who works the front desk to the chief executive officer—should receive annual information technology security training, not just the IT team. The reason for this, which many people don't like to believe, is that information technology security and protecting the company from computer-related threats is everyone's job, not just the job of the IT team.

If security were left to the information technology team, and the office users didn't have to worry about security at all, one of two things would happen:

1. The company would be taken over by viruses and ransomware within a short period of time.

2. The desktop computers and network would be so locked down that the users wouldn't be able to do anything, probably including their job.

As neither of those outcomes will allow the company to have its employees working at their full potential, a solution needs to be put in place, which is to have all the employees take information technology security seriously.

This security training isn't something that can be done once and then we can assume that the employee will remember the training forever. The threats that employees face day to day through email or text messaging can and will change over time, and new attack vectors will be found and exploited. Because of this alone, the training needs to be refreshed and presented to the user regularly (typically annually) in order to show them the new attacks they could face and how to respond to them. Additionally, the information from years past needs to be regularly reinforced as people will often forget it.

While we would like to assume that everyone will be able to spot SPAM and scam messages that come in, they won't. Referring to the Internet Crime Report of 2017, which is available at https://egits4smb.com/go/ic3, we can see that a huge amount of money was taken from people in a single year, as shown in Table 9-1.

Table 9-1. Amounts Reported in the Internet Crime Report of 2017

Theft Category	Loss Amount (in Millions of Dollars)
Real Estate / Rental	56
Corporate Data Breach	60
Non-Payment / Non-Delivery	141
Personal Data Breach	77
Credit Card Fraud	57
Email Compromise	676
Identity Theft	66
Advance Fee	57
Investment	96
Confidence Fraud / Romance	211
Total	1,497

As you can see from the amounts shown in Table 9-1, it is estimated that ~$1.5 billion was scammed from people and companies in just one year. And, sadly, that estimate is probably pretty low, and those are just the victims who were willing to come forward and say that they got scammed.

Many victims are too embarrassed or too afraid to report to the authorities that they were scammed. The fear is often justified. Once people figure out that they've been scammed and they try to get their money back from the scammer, the scammer will often threaten them with violence in order to keep them from talking to the press or the authorities. And all too often, the threats work.

Risks of Not Doing Regular Training

By not doing regular training, the company runs the risk of not having their employees aware of the latest trends and the latest vectors that attackers can use, which may directly affect them. There is an old adage in the IT field:

> CEO: What if we pay to train these employees and they leave?CTO: What if we don't pay to train them, and they stay?

> —Unknown

Normally this is talking about training information technology[3] workers so that they are trained with the newer skills, but in this case it applies to everyone at the company. If the company doesn't pay for training, the risk is that the employee does something that can put the livelihood of the company at risk. And that risk is then spread to every employee at the company, all because one malicious link was clicked on, or one email was responded to. In the worst case, a single untrained employee could cause the entire company to close.

With that potential outcome in play, spending a little money on employee training every year just seems like the responsible thing for the company to do. The cost of the training, in some cases, can be offset by lower cyber-insurance rates. Some certifications may even require that some or all employees receive this sort of training, and some clients may require some sort of training as well. And if the company is going to spend the time and money to buy or build this training for a few employees, presenting it to all the employees should cost very little to nothing more.

Least Privilege

The concept of least privilege (which was alluded to earlier in this chapter) is a concept in information technology where the person has access to the various systems they need access to, but no more access beyond that. This means that we don't give every user of the customer management system administrative rights in that system.

---

[3] More can be read about the perils of not training information technology workers at https://www.egits4smb.com/go/inc.

If an employee's role is to look up customers and create tickets when those customers call in, that is the only access to the system they should get. If the employee doesn't need access to create or update a customer's information, then they don't get that level of access. If they don't need to see the customer's address, then those fields are blanked out. This minimizes the attack surface that can be used to take customer data.

Fully deploying the concept of least privilege will take planning, and probably ruffle a few feathers of employees who have been at the company for a while, as well as the executives.

Employees who have been at the company a while are going to see the access that they have in the system as that needed to do their job. And if they do need extra access, then the access to those fields or systems should be given back. If, however, they only want that access because they have always had it, that is not a good enough reason to restore the access. It needs to be explained that the change isn't to punish them or because they did something wrong. The change is to protect them so that if an attacker were to break into the company's systems using their credentials, the attacker wouldn't be able to get access to what they were looking for.

With executives, the information technology team can be in a difficult situation. In this case, the IT team needs to tell their boss that they don't need to be able to access some system, or some data. Looking at the prior example of a customer management system, does the IT director really need to be able to log in to the customer management system to pull up customer information? No, they probably don't, so that access should be taken away from them.

It can be hard to explain to executives why they don't have access to everything in the company, especially for small companies where the executives in question own the company. In some situations, the IT team can use regulatory or compliance reasons to justify the need to remove access. But it needs to be done; these executives need to be protected from themselves. By insisting that they have access to everything within the company, they are making themselves a target so that an attacker can breach their credentials and gain access to resources within the company.

Protecting Secrets

Secrets in the information technology field are a fancy, all-encompassing term for passwords, encryption keys, certificates, basically anything that is used to gain access to a protected system, such as a database or application programming interface (API).

The problem with these secrets is that they have to be put into something in order for them to be used. Typically, this will be a configuration file for an application. And this will then make it very easy to read the secret. Beyond the fact that the secret can be easily read at this point, there is the issue that the secret can be accidently checked into source control, where it is kept forever.

If your company uses a private source control, this is less of a problem, but still is a problem. If your company is using a public source control provider, such as GitHub, and your source code repositories are public, this can lead to all sorts of problems, depending on what the secret is.

There are horror stories of people checking the API codes that allow them to interface with their AWS environment into GitHub, into a public repository. This effectively allows anyone to download the API key and have access to their AWS environment.

You are probably asking yourself, but who's going to look in some random person's repository for this key? The answer to that is automated scripts. These automated scripts are looking at GitHub (and other public source control repositories), searching for API keys that will give them access to the cloud platforms and, most important, have other people pay for it.

One such example can be found online at `https://www.egits4smb.com/go/keys`. A person was taking an online class on a programming language called Ruby on Rails. As part of the class, he needed to view a spreadsheet that had the API keys in it. These API keys are essentially passwords. As part of the class, he accidently uploaded the spreadsheet to GitHub. There is a team at GitHub whose job it is to look for people accidently posting secrets to their cloud accounts. This team contacted the user and told him about the potential problem. By the time he logged into his AWS account to stop the access, the attacker had already spun up several resources and spent over $3,000 in just a few days, with a projected spend for just that month of about $15,000.

Thankfully, the GitHub team was able to contact him quickly and help resolve the problem (with the help of AWS personnel as well, as talked about in the article).

But what would have happened if GitHub hadn't contacted him? And what if he was a decent-sized company, not just a person? Having those resources up and running could have taken months to find, and potentially could have cost tens or hundreds of thousands of dollars.

Secrets, basically no matter what kind they are, should always be stored in a secret management platform. Microsoft Azure has one called Azure Key Vault. Amazon AWS has one called AWS KMS, and Google's GCP has one called Cloud Key Management. There are lots on on-premises solutions as well, with solutions called enterprise key managers (EKMs). No matter which one is used, they all perform basically the same function. They provide you with a secure place to store secrets so that they can be retrieved by only the machine that is supposed to retrieve them.

Using Azure Key Vault, for example, each virtual machine can be assigned an identity. That identity is then given access to the Azure Key Vault and is allowed (using the concept of least privilege) to pull down the secrets that it needs. In the case of Azure Key Vault, we would give the virtual machine access to get the secret, but not to list the secrets. This way, if the virtual machine were compromised, they attacker wouldn't be able to log in to the Key Vault to get the list of secrets and then download them. They could only download the secrets when they knew the actual name of the secret.

This way, if and when the configuration file is checked in by accident, the secret isn't exposed, as the secret is safely stored in Azure Key Vault.

Employee Training

People are the weakest link when it comes to attackers' getting access to the company's internal network. To prevent employees' being used to gain access to the company's network, those employees need to be trained on spotting the ways in which attackers will attempt to use them to gain access to company systems.

Passwords

The first thing about passwords that employees need to know is that they should never, under any circumstances, share their password with anyone else. Along with that, help-desk personnel should be trained to never ask employees for their passwords. If help-desk workers ask employees for their passwords, even occasionally, the employees will become used to giving out their passwords, and it is a reasonable assumption that an employee will give out their password to an attacker who is pretending to be a help-desk employee.

The same rule applies to the codes that are used for multi-factor authentication (MFA). These codes should never be shared with other people. If an employee receives multi-factor authentication requests (either an approval request, as

D. Cherry, *Enterprise-Grade IT Security for Small and Medium Businesses*,
https://doi.org/10.1007/978-1-4842-8628-9_10

shown in Figure 10-1 via a multi-factor authentication application, or an authentication code sent via text message) that the employee didn't trigger themselves, they should assume that their account is compromised.

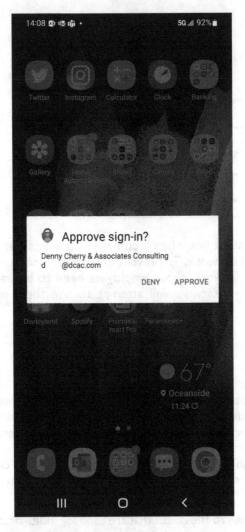

Figure 10-1. Multi-factor authentication approval prompt

When it comes to changing their passwords, people need to pick a password that is hard for a computer to guess (meaning that the password needs to be long), but easy for the employee to remember, so that they don't write their password down on a piece of paper.

It is common for people to write their password down, put it on a Post-it note, and hide the note under their keyboard, or in some situations even post the note on their monitor.

The trick when selecting a password is to select a password that is easy to remember but long enough that it is basically impossible to guess. The easiest way for people to do this is to use a pass phrase instead of a password. This involves using a sentence, or part of a sentence, as the password instead of just a single word. While a password might look like "B@ndQu33n," a pass phrase could look like "TheB@ndQu33nIsF@nt@stIc". Long passwords can have their own problems. Many systems or websites set maximum password limits, often short ones. These requirements for short passwords end up being a security risk, and should cause concern, as who knows what other poor security processes they have.

While the password "B@ndQu33n" isn't bad, as it has all four of the character types (uppercase letter, lowercase letters, numbers, and special characters), it is shorter than it could be. Because it is just nine characters it would take a relatively short period of time for a computer to brute force this password. The pass phrase in question started as "The Band Queen is Fantastic," and once we remove the spaces and switch a few characters into numbers and characters we end up with the phrase "TheB@ndQu33nIsF@nt@stIc".

The easiest way to swap letters to numbers is to switch "e" to "3" and "i" to "I". For some added security, and to ensure that the phrase will take even longer to brute force, we can swap out the "a" with an "@" symbol. This gives us a phrase that is 23 characters long, uses all four character types, and would take effectively forever to brute force, while being relatively easy for the user to remember. There are questions out there about whether symbols should be used in a password or not. By including symbols in the password the potential number of characters available increases two-fold, which increases the amount of time that would be needed to brute force the password.

Different systems allow for different symbols to be used. Some systems allow for the basic symbols (the ones above the numbers of a standard U.S. keyboard). Other systems allow for all potential characters, such as the smiley face symbol ☺.

Employees probably don't understand that this is a great way to come up with secure passwords that are safe from attackers and from brute forcing. Most people don't know that they can use this technique to choose passwords that are more safe and secure. When people are taught not just the how, but also the why of creating good, secure passwords, they will take the process much more seriously than if you just tell them how to create secure passwords.

Phishing

Phishing (fishing) emails are emails that are sent out en masse, generally without any true personalization of the emails. Because they are sent out to a wide group of people, typically tens of thousands or hundreds of thousands of people, often the "To" field of these emails will be empty, as shown in Figure 10-2, or the it will be the same (or similar) to the "From" field, as shown in Figure 10-3.

Unclaimed Inheritance Fund 1

DESMOND&ASSOCIATE CH/
To

Figure 10-2. A SPAM email with a blank "To" field

Agnes Chan Jeah Yee <agnes.ch
To ○Agnes Chan Jeah Yee

Figure 10-3. A SPAM email with the same account in both the "From" field and the "To" field

These phishing emails don't always look obvious. The sender is looking to collect one of three different kinds of information from the victim:

1. Banking information

2. Personal information

3. Login details

Banking Information

This happens when a phisher sends out emails saying that the victim has won some sort of lottery or inheritance, or is asked to help move money between countries. An example of a phishing email where the end result is the phisher looking for banking information is shown in Figure 10-4.

COMPENSATION PAYMENT FOR 2021 FISCAL YEAR:

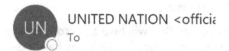

UNITED NATION <officia   @gmail.com>
To

Dear Sir/Ma Good day,

COMPENSATION PAYMENT FOR 2021 FISCAL YEAR:

Sorry for making this contact through e-mail since we could not reach your phone number.

My name is Mr Antonio Guterrez,Secretary to United Nations.
A meeting was held on your behalf by just concluded 73rd United Nation's general assembly within the UN/IMF countries concerning the unclaimed funds denied to many people all over the world. Your funds will be release to you by the paying bank for immediate payment .it was discovered during this meeting that no funds has been paid to you all this years of pursuit.The funds is now ready to be release to you since you have been approved to receive/claim this compensation payment of $15Million ($15 000,000.00 USD).

We have instructions to release your payment to you.

Kindly Forward Your

Names,
Address,
Telephone Number,
Next of Kin and Occupation

for the release of your payment. The UN is sorry for the delay of funds release.

Figure 10-4. *Sample phishing email*

While the sample email shown in Figure 10-4 isn't specifically asking for banking information, if this email were responded to, the phisher would eventually ask for a fee to be paid for the transfer.

There are a few different items within this email that will help a person identify it as a phishing email looking for banking information. These items have been circled in Figure 10-5.

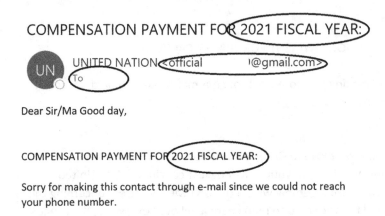

COMPENSATION PAYMENT FOR 2021 FISCAL YEAR:

UNITED NATION<official   l@gmail.com>
To

Dear Sir/Ma Good day,

COMPENSATION PAYMENT FOR 2021 FISCAL YEAR:

Sorry for making this contact through e-mail since we could not reach your phone number.

My name is Mr Antonio Guterrez,Secretary to United Nations. A meeting was held on your behalf by just concluded 73rd United Nation's general assembly within the UN/IMF countries concerning the unclaimed funds denied to many people all over the world. Your funds will be release to you by the paying bank for immediate payment .it was discovered during this meeting that no funds has been paid to you all this years of pursuit.The funds is now ready to be release to you since you have been approved to receive/claim this compensation payment of $15Million ($15 000,000.00 USD).

We have instructions to release your payment to you.

Kindly Forward Your

Names,
Address,
Telephone Number,
Next of Kin and Occupation

for the release of your payment. The UN is sorry for the delay of funds release.

Figure 10-5. Sample phishing email with warning signs circled

The most obvious problems with this email are shown in the "From" and "To" fields. The "From" field shows a generic email address from Gmail. Official emails from the United Nations wouldn't come from a gmail.com email address; they would come from un.org, in this case. Additionally, the "To" field wouldn't be blank. The next problem that identifies it as a phishing email is the subject line (at the top, as this was in Microsoft Outlook), as well as the first line. Both of these indicate the 2021 Fiscal Year, but the email was received in 2022 (the UN fiscal year runs on a calendar year).

The next reason to think that this email is a potential phishing email is due to the misspelling in the body of the email. The phrase "this years of pursuit" makes no sense to a native English speaker.

The final hint that this is a phishing email is that it asked for the name, address, phone number, and next of kin of the sender. If this were a legitimate email, the sender would already know at least your name, if not your address and phone number. If this were a legitimate offer of a wire transfer, there would be no need to know anything about your next of kin.

Personal Information

Phishing emails can attempt to get personal information about the recipient as well. Phishers can ask for anything—the trick is training employees not to give it to them. Phishers ask for this information because they've been successful in the past. Phishers will ask for people to send their Social Security number (the United States' version of a Tax ID number), name, address, phone number, passport number, etc.

These phishing emails are designed to collect personal information in order for the attacker to be able to create a false identify using the information of the employee. This could lead to the phisher's being able to create fake passports, register for credit cards in the name of the employee, open bank accounts, refinance or sell property such as the employee's house, and more.

Social media can be a treasure trove of information, as many people will post the answers to many security questions on their social media. This includes answering surveys on social media, often with the answers publicly posted. While the answers to these surveys don't have the person's password, they do have many of the answers to the needed security questions at work, or the person's bank, etc.

Login Details

Another piece of information that an attacker wants to gain access to is the credentials of the employee in question. These emails will typically say that your password has expired or that you are out of storage space for your email account, but by clicking the link in the email you can resolve this issue, such as in the email shown in Figure 10-6.

From: AdminNotice-dcac.com <twostep-noreply@wba.com>
Sent on: Thursday, April 14, 2022 7:14:37 PM
To: k   .com
Subject: Your Storage Is Almost Exceeding The Limit

Microsoft 365

Hi kris,

Storage Used 97%

You have less than 3% of your k   .com storage space and 7 undelivered messages. If you run out of storage space you will not be able to send or receive messages from Thursday, April 14, 2022.

You should clear cache to release pending emails and free some space .

CLEAR CACHE

Figure 10-6. *Sample email to capture login details*

After clicking the link in the email shown in Figure 10-6, the employee will be taken to a web page that looks similar to the Microsoft 365 login screen, but is actually hosted on a compromised website.

After the employee enters their Microsoft 365 credentials, the attacker either captures the login information, or the website is configured in such a way that it automatically logs in to the Microsoft 365 platform and downloads the user's contact information, sending a similar phishing email to everyone in the employee's contact list.

The attacker will typically keep the login information so that they can perform additional actions as the employee, which only works if the employee doesn't have multi-factor authentication enabled, or until the employee changes their password.

Spear Phishing

Spear phishing is similar to phishing attacks. The difference is that while general phishing attacks are sent to a large number of people, spear phishing attacks are targeted against a specific individual. Like the email shown in Figure 10-6, spear phishing emails include specific information about a specific employee, including items such as the employee's name and email address or other information, such as the city they live in, as circled in Figure 10-7.

From: AdminNotice-dcac.com <twostep-noreply@wba.com>

Sent on: Thursday, April 14, 2022 7:14:37 PM

To: k   .com

Subject: Your Storage Is Almost Exceeding The Limit

Microsoft 365

Hi kris,

Storage Used 97%

You have less than 3% of your   .com storage space and 7 undelivered messages. If you run out of storage space you will not be able to send or receive messages from Thursday, April 14, 2022.

You should clear cache to release pending emails and free some space .

CLEAR CACHE

Figure 10-7. *Sample spear phishing email with customizations highlighted*

As you can see in Figure 10-7, the email attempts to look like an official email coming from Microsoft. However, the email address from which this was sent is not a Microsoft.com email address. An official email from Microsoft would also include the Microsoft logo. In addition to this, it is suspicious that the email says that seven emails are undelivered and gives a date after which email will not be able to be sent and received, even though there is still free space (not to mention the grammatical error in the sentence with the date).

Cat Phishing

Cat phishing, while sounding like phishing and spear phishing, is a totally different attack vector. Cat phishing is a method of getting information out of people while the attacker pretends to be someone other than who they are.

Typically, the cat phishing perpetrator pretends to be a young attractive person, of whichever gender the victim prefers, usually pretending to be a 20-something-year-old. Using this person, an attacker will attempt to convince the victim to send wire transfers of money in exchange for virtual sex messages, possibly using pictures of a young person who matches the physical description the attacker has given the victim.

The attacker may even convince the victim to perform sex acts on camera for the supposed pleasure of the attacker, all while the attacker records the video of the victim.

This recording gives the attacker leverage over the victim, allowing the attacker to force the victim into giving the attacker money or information beyond what the victim normally would.

The normal threat against the victim will be that the attacker will release the video if the victim doesn't give the attacker what they ask for. Typically this will be money, or information about the company the victim works for.

While cat-phishing attacks take time and will cost the attacker money to keep up appearances, it can pay off if the attacker gets a victim with money or access. Things become even more dangerous for the victim if they don't have money or information, as the attacker can convince the victim to take out loans to get the money, or to take out another mortgage on their house in order to send the attacker money.

The most successful cat phishing attacks involve the victim's not knowing that they are being tricked into sending money and information. If the attacker can convince the victim to do something illegal (or that appears to be illegal), the attacker will hold the threat of telling the authorities about what was done in order to convince the victim do to more things that are illegal or that would further compromise the victim and/or the company for which they work.

Cat phishing sometimes starts with an email that is sent to the victim. More often than not, it starts in an internet chat room where the attacker pretends to be just another person looking for companionship, which they can spin into a successful cat phishing attack.

Fake Links

Almost all emails designed to steal information will include some sort of link. By referring the victim to a website, the cost to the attacker drops dramatically compared to the cost of having the potential victims reply to an email address. The biggest risk to their scam operation, when the victims need to email the scammer back, is that the email address could be closed, assuming that it is hosted on a public service like Gmail or Hotmail. When the attacker has a custom domain name, they risk that the domain could be seized by law enforcement.

If we look closer at the link shown in Figure 10-6, we can hover over the link and see where the link is pointing. While a true email from Microsoft will point to a domain owned by Microsoft, usually a microsoft.com or aka.ms (another domain owned by Microsoft), a phishing email will have a link that points, as shown in Figure 10-8, to a third-party domain, in this case ending in vip.cl, which is, needless to say, not a Microsoft domain.

Figure 10-8. A link pretending to be from Microsoft

During training, employees need to be taught to hover their mouse over links in emails they receive before they click on the link to ensure that the link points to where it is expected to go. If links point to unexpected domains, like the one shown in Figure 10-8, they should be identified before the user clicks on the link.

In the case of the link shown in Figure 10-8, going to this link directs the user to another website, which in this case prompts the user to authenticate with their Microsoft 365 account.

Fake Receipts

One of the newest methods which attackers are using to attempt to steal money from their victims is via the issuance of fake receipts to the victim. These emails make it look like the victim has purchased some product from the attacker, either through eBay, Dell, Microsoft, Norton or any other legitimate company.

As you can see in Figure 10-9, the attacker has sent an email to the victim stating that the victim's debit card has been charged. By checking the bank's website, the victim can see that there is no charge as the attacker does not yet have your credit card or debit card information.

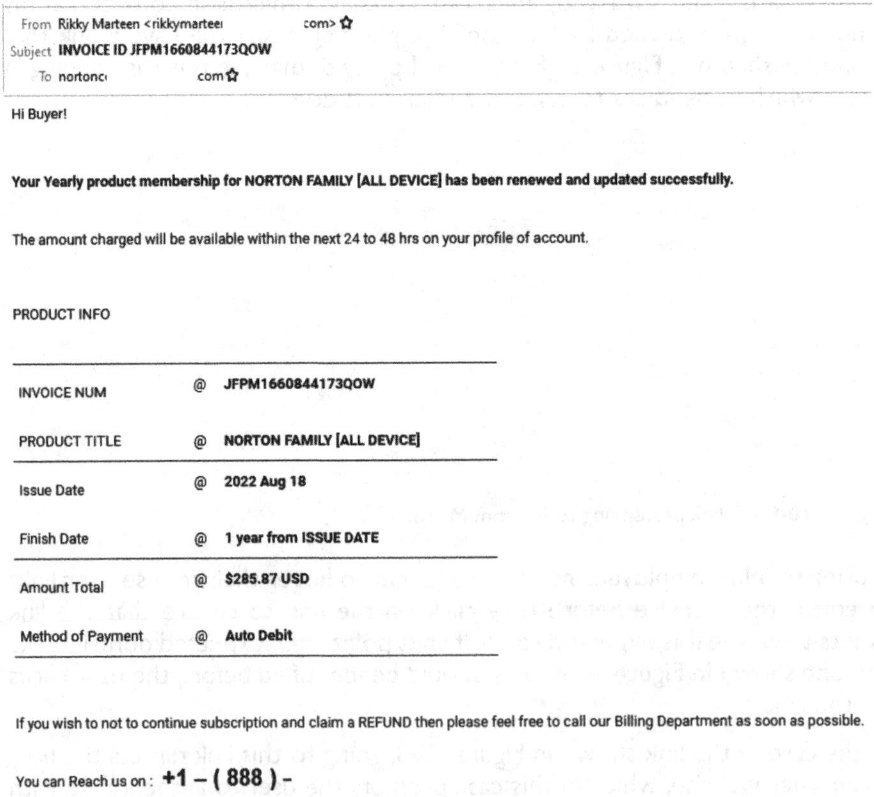

From Rikky Marteen <rikkymarteei   com> ☆

Subject **INVOICE ID JFPM1660844173QOW**

To nortonc   com ☆

Hi Buyer!

Your Yearly product membership for NORTON FAMILY [ALL DEVICE] has been renewed and updated successfully.

The amount charged will be available within the next 24 to 48 hrs on your profile of account.

PRODUCT INFO

INVOICE NUM	@	**JFPM1660844173QOW**
PRODUCT TITLE	@	**NORTON FAMILY [ALL DEVICE]**
Issue Date	@	**2022 Aug 18**
Finish Date	@	**1 year from ISSUE DATE**
Amount Total	@	**$285.87 USD**
Method of Payment	@	**Auto Debit**

If you wish to not to continue subscription and claim a REFUND then please feel free to call our Billing Department as soon as possible.

You can Reach us on : **+1 – (888) –**

Figure 10-9. SPAM email attempting to get the victim to call the attacker for a refund

The attacker's goal at this point is to get the victim to call the attacker at the phone number which they have provided. When the victim calls, the attacker will be very contrite and explain how this shouldn't have happened and that they will need to process a refund. But because of the security of their system, they can't refund the money to the credit card that was used because their system doesn't let them see the card, so they can't refund without the card number.

Once the victim gives them a credit card number, expiration date, and security code from the credit card, the attacker will charge that credit card as much as they can before the card begins to decline the charges.

If the card which the attacker is given is a debit card linked to a bank account, that means that the attacker will have drained the account, and they will continue to do so each time money is deposited into the account until the debit card is closed. If the card is a credit card, the attacker will simply run up the credit card until the card reaches the spending limit of the credit card.

No matter what kind of card is used by the victim, the victim will need to work with the bank or credit card institution which issued the card in order to reverse whatever charges can be reversed.

Inbound Email Security

There are a variety of email security platforms available that review emails when they are received. These platforms process the email headers as well as the content of the email to ensure, with a decent degree of accuracy, that the emails are safe for the end users.

These platforms are configurable and allow the sensitivity to be increased or decreased based on the number of false positives or negatives the company deems acceptable. If the settings are too sensitive, valid emails will be marked as SPAM, phishing, or scams. If the settings are not sensitive enough, then some SPAM, phishing, or scam emails will make their way through the filter. There is no way to guarantee that there will be no scam emails as well as no false positives. However, the settings can be fine-tuned to minimize the number of SPAM emails that get past the filters.

Because some SPAM emails will always get through the filters, no matter what the sales representatives for the SPAM filters say, users need to be trained to spot the fake emails in order to ensure that the problem emails are not clicked on.

Index

I

Printed in the United States
by Baker & Taylor Publisher Services

Printed in the United States
by Baker & Taylor Publisher Services